D1765169

C016015226

ABIGAIL AHERN
COLOUR.

BANISH BEIGE.
BOOST COLOUR.
TRANSFORM YOUR HOME.

PHOTOGRAPHY BY
GRAHAM ATKINS-HUGHES

QUADRILLE

CONTENTS

INTRODUCTION

Colour is clever. Get it right and it lifts your spirits, get it wrong and it will make you run for the hills! It has been my obsession for as far back as I can remember. I grew up in a colourful home. My mother, an artist, would choose shades for our walls in the same way that she would select colours for her paintings: instinctively, from feeling and observation.

I remember, from a young age, ox blood on the walls in the living room; a forest green dining room; accents of blues and purples; black floors; rich, often chalky finishes that offset my mother's paintings beautifully. Friends and neighbours would come over and think our house a little odd and, conversely, we would think the same about theirs. Why, we mused, was everyone so hesitant when it came to applying colour to their homes?

Of course, I rebelled. In my early twenties, I landed a job in London working for Sir Terence Conran's publishing company, with a seriously cool crowd. I had just moved out of home and was done with that Victorian colour palette – so old-fashioned, I thought. I wanted to rock what everyone else was rocking: Scandi simplicity, white everything; minimal, functional and, now I look back, beyond boring!

Fast-forward a few years and I met my now husband, Graham, who landed a job in America. We were living in a rental and not allowed to paint a thing, so I started to dabble with adding vitality to the rental through colour, pattern and texture. Gradually my confidence with colour grew. We returned to London, bought a dilapidated four-storey townhouse and it was here (where I remain today) that my confidence with colour gained new heights.

Initially I did what everyone else does: I painted the whole thing out in white. Then I got bored and started experimenting with some darker hues, not dissimilar to the ones I had grown up with, although altogether much deeper.

I remember feeling cocooned, protected and very much loved in my parents' house. I didn't get that vibe in my minimal London townhouse and I so wanted to capture it again. What's more, I missed America. I was all at sea as to what I wanted to do for a career and, quite frankly, I wasn't very happy in my new white home So I started experimenting.

I began by painting walls out light grey, but they felt too pale. I moved to dark grey. This lasted for about three years but, still, it wasn't dark enough. So I took the plunge and went black. The day I did, magic struck. I fell in love. The intensity was transformative!

I did the very same thing in my store and then strange things began to happen. For a start, the paint job got us a ton of press coverage. The house was photographed and the photographs got sold around the world 60 times over. Celebs would fly in from all over and the one thing everyone commented on was the colour of the walls. I knew I was onto something!

WHAT COLOUR BRINGS

The ability of colour to transform surroundings, to excite, inspire, tantalise and calm, is second to none. It has changed my life. I know this sounds super dramatic but it's true. Colour has given me a home that I never want to leave. It has made me happier. When I put my key in the door at the end of a long day I get this squishy feeling of contentment that envelopes me, and it is all because of colour. I can assure you, a white hallway just wouldn't have the same effect!

The photographs in this book come from homes across the globe which display a virtuosic talent for colour. They range confidently from hushed tones – muted and complex, drawn from ocean-front or woodland settings – to intense colour-saturated spaces, akin to something you would find in a Technicolor musical. Throw in shots of glistening blues, Amazon parrot green, blingy gold, purple and cobalt, and it's an inspiring selection that is beyond beautiful.

The colours on show here are not 'on trend', they are timeless, sophisticated combos that you will want to live with forever (rather than change up every 15 minutes). No sherbet lemons and baby blues in this book!

FIGURING OUT YOUR STYLE DNA

My motto in life is to take risks. Simply put, you can't create a jaw-on-the-floor interior without them. So I want this book to make you think a little differently about colour and stop being scared.

I'm not going to bang on about scientific theories or bore you with rules. I'm a strong believer that you should choose colour from a feeling. But I do want to push you out of your comfort zone. In all my years in the biz, I've found clients remarkably hesitant when it comes to applying colour in their homes. It's natural to want to cling to your tried-and-trusted hues, the safe solutions (or 'non-colours', as I like to call them). Yet whenever I hold one of my Design Classes at home, the next week I am flooded with emails from students who have converted to the dark side.

The best news is that boring old magnolia is losing some of its attraction, with more people willing to experiment with different hues, from dark to bright. I ran a poll across my social media channels not so long ago and was blown away by the many confident colour choices that people are making!

You do need a dose of confidence when it comes to colour, but that's the easy part. My first chapter will lead you through the choices and help you create a palette that is personal to you.

Chapter two is packed with the most magical colour combinations. Grasp the effect different colours have on each other, and you can mix them up, clash, block, blend or pop – with dazzling results!

Few of us are born with an instinctive sense of colour. More often than not, it's learned. In chapter three, I'll walk you through building colour into your home, with the help of texture, pattern, lighting, furniture and greenery.

In chapter four we'll get down to specifics, running through each and every room in the house. Aspirational, amazing ideas for entryways, living rooms, dining rooms, bedrooms, bathrooms, kitchens, studies and even outdoor spaces.

Next up, I'll be encouraging you to Be Audacious, by drilling down into all those small decisions that take your home to the next level. And the last chapter? That's dedicated to paint: the easiest, cheapest, best decorating tool around.

Excited?

Me too. Let's get going!

THE
COLOUR
CHALLE

NGE

HOW TO STOP PROCRASTINATING ABOUT COLOUR

Pushing your colour choices will utterly reinvent your space, turning it into a place you will never want to leave. The trick is not to be afraid!

I SUFFERED FROM COLOUR PARALYSIS FOR YEARS. Deciding on the paint colour for one room is hard enough, let alone figuring out a palette for the whole house. Will your chosen hues work together? Should they harmonise, clash, contrast?

EVERYTHING CHANGED WHEN I STARTED EXPERIMENTING, DABBLING IN NEW SHADES, TAKING A FEW RISKS. Nowadays, my approach to colour is super simple. Forget expensive colour consultations and instead look upon colour as you would the prospect of conjuring up a delicious meal. Each colour (ingredient) has a different flavour profile; each can be combined to tantalising effect.

RATHER THAN PLAYING IT SAFE (AS WE ARE ALL INCLINED TO DO) PUSH OUT OF YOUR COMFORT ZONE. I know this isn't easy. Last year, for example, I decided to change the colour palette throughout our house. Everything was painted grey, but I wanted each room to have a different hue, whilst still aiming for a cohesive palette. It was one of the hardest decorating decisions I've ever made. Accessories that I thought would work in each space didn't sit right with the new palette. Rugs, lights, flowers, furniture – nothing stayed put. Luckily most of this stuff only moved rooms, but it took a while to get things right and it's still not 100 per cent there.

BUT I LIKE HOW IT'S MAKING ME THINK. I like how shades I have never loved or used, had previously overlooked or dismissed – purple reddish tones like plum and grape – are entering my life. I like how they are making me think differently. The truth is, the more colour risks you take, the more intriguing your space will look. It really is life changing!

When it comes to colouring your home try going outside the lines. One of the best ways to expand a space is by using sharp shots of colour, like this amazing green on the walls and the turquoise chair.

The colour palette that Kelly Wearstler has used in her Malibu beachhouse is one of the most beautiful and complex I've ever seen. Inspired by a natural palette – silvery greys, driftwood taupes, watery greens and storm cloud greys – it's what you might call glammed-up neutrals. I adore!

FINDING COLOUR INSPIRATION

If you have no idea where to start on your colour scheme, the best, simplest advice I can give you is to follow your gut. When I decorate, I don't get hung up on particulars, like the amount of natural light in a space, the architecture, the size of a room or its orientation. Instead, use your natural intuition when it comes to selecting colours and make sure they are personally right for you.

CREATE A MOODBOARD.
Start by pulling together images out of magazines, screen grabs and swatches that instantly appeal, to see if a common theme arises (for a list of my favourite sources, turn to page 236).

PICK COLOURS THAT SUIT YOUR PERSONALITY.
And don't listen to anybody other than yourself when selecting a palette. (You can be sure I don't!) Once you tell friends or family about your new colour plans, you'll get all those old clichés thrown at you: 'blue is cold'; 'red and orange clash'; 'blue and green should never be seen'. Actually, the more you ditch the old rules and decorate from your heart, the cooler your pad will look.

SHOP YOUR HOME.
By which I mean, look at the colours you already live with, from the clothes in your wardrobe to a large piece of art or your favourite rug. If you find you gravitate to certain hues, reflect these in your decorating scheme.

KEEP YOUR EYES PEELED.
Inspiration can come from anywhere. For me, oftentimes it is literally on my doorstop. I've had a love affair with grey for as far back as I can remember. It's all those saucepan-lid grey London skies. I love them! Then again, the colours in my latest paint range – tobaccos; noirs; inky blues; earthy reds, shots of bold teals and jungle greens – came from my time living in Manhattan, NYC, with its hub of Kafkaesque hangouts, unsanctioned street art and hipster counterculture. It's an effortlessly cool palette that I really gravitate towards.

IF ALL ELSE FAILS, FIND INSPIRATION IN NATURE.
Colours that appear in nature will always work indoors and it takes the thinking out!

TEN WAYS TO COLOUR CONFIDENCE

1 Start by picking a colour for your biggest room – say your living room or kitchen. Choose a hue that feels beautiful and inspiring, and true to what you love. Build on this to create a limited palette of colours for your entire home, using different combinations of those colours in each room.

2 Use an existing feature in your pad to inspire the basis of your colour scheme. This could be a view from the window, a work of art or any favourite item you own.

3 Think about what you want your home to communicate to the outside world. No one will be talking about your beige-on-beige home, so go a little crazy. Be reckless, I say! The more your confidence grows, the more you'll feel like experimenting with colour.

4 Be brave! To start with, decorating with colour can seem like a daunting task. Colour behaves differently according to where you put it. The effect changes again once you add lighting, pattern, texture and greenery into the mix. I think this is why people favour whites over any other colour group, as they distort less when other elements are thrown into the mix. However, to me, this is a bit like decorating by numbers. Too easy! Bold hues, on the other hand, make everything on display feel grander, cooler, more intense, with beautiful undertones subtly changing in the daylight. You'll never look back!

Remember, there are no no-nos. Well almost none. Pastels are one grouping I never want to work with. But then plop me in Miami and I'm sure I'd be instantly seduced!

Use colour in unexpected places: behind closed doors, inside kitchen cupboards, bedroom wardrobes, the loo – all those tucked away places that surprise the minute you enter (see page 33).

Remember the small stuff. Introduce colour through cushions, vases, bowls, fruit, greenery – you name it. There should be splashes everywhere for your eye to alight on!

All colour schemes are improved by accents: the final touches of colour that add an element of surprise, and bring rooms to life. There are no fixed rules when it comes to choosing these; just take care with the amount of colour you use and where you use it. As fab as that bright orange might look on a pillow, it may not feel quite so amazing on four walls because the impact will be so much stronger.

Patterns provide necessary punctuation; don't neglect them. They anchor a space like nothing else I know (see pages 95–8).

Create the illusion of space by blurring the boundaries between walls and ceilings. Paint them all out the same colour and suddenly you've made your space a zillion times bigger. Promise!

BALANCE THE MIX

The biggest tip I can give you when selecting a palette is to nail the mood or atmosphere you want to create first. Do that, and figuring out what colour to go for gets so much easier.

Let's say you fancy a calm, serene bedroom. You'll want a colour palette that acts as a backdrop rather than a focal point. In which case, consider some easy-on-the-eye shades: quarry, bone, linen, pewter. Neutrals provide the perfect foundation for any style (turn to page 58 to see how it's done).

I love strong shots of bad boy hues, but a little colour goes a long way, so rein it in. I instinctively limit my palate to three colours, to prevent things from becoming too crazy and disconnected. If you use multiple tones of the same hue, it will pull the scheme together beautifully.

Don't have every piece fighting for attention with a different hue. When decorating eclectically, a few neutrals will quietly finish the job, harmonising, unifying and letting any oddball hues take centre stage.

Group similar coloured accessories together to give your space an impactful and non-permanent pop of interest. Adding colour can be as simple as adding a plant, or as full-on as adding a huge rug (page 203).

Bohemian cushions with a south-of-the-border vibe dress up the leather sofa, lending a colourful vibrancy to this living space.

You can paint a room
in any hue you like
if you stick to just
three rules ...

MAKE IT PERSONAL.

TAKE RISKS.

BE CURIOUS.

FIGURING THIS OUT THAN YOU

Start small. You don't need to repaint your walls, or even go down the furniture route. A vase, a throw, even a painting on the wall will elevate, uplift and pack a visual punch. The more confident you get, the bigger and bolder you can take it.

Accent with off-radar hues – blush, peach, pinky red – to add a different perspective to your space. Or use oddball hues – yellow, burnt orange, a shocking electric blue – to lift the heart, liberate inhibitions and show the world that you are not over-the-hill and crusty. I use orange as an accent on trays, vases, flowers – it's a really fun hue to bounce around.

Distribute colour around the room so there's a lively rhythm going on. I'm obsessed with the visual contrast of warm and cool tones (see pages 34 and 218–9); it's that friction that creates tension and that tension that creates magic.

If you want to update anything, add an injection of black. Its deep saturation creates instant depth and visual intrigue. I'm obsessed!

Right: You don't have to overdose on colour to take your pad to the next level. Layer on texture instead! Think rich woods, plaid wallpapers, a funky chair. All the pieces in this vignette are shouting from a similar colour palette – warm neutrals – and the effect is fabulous!

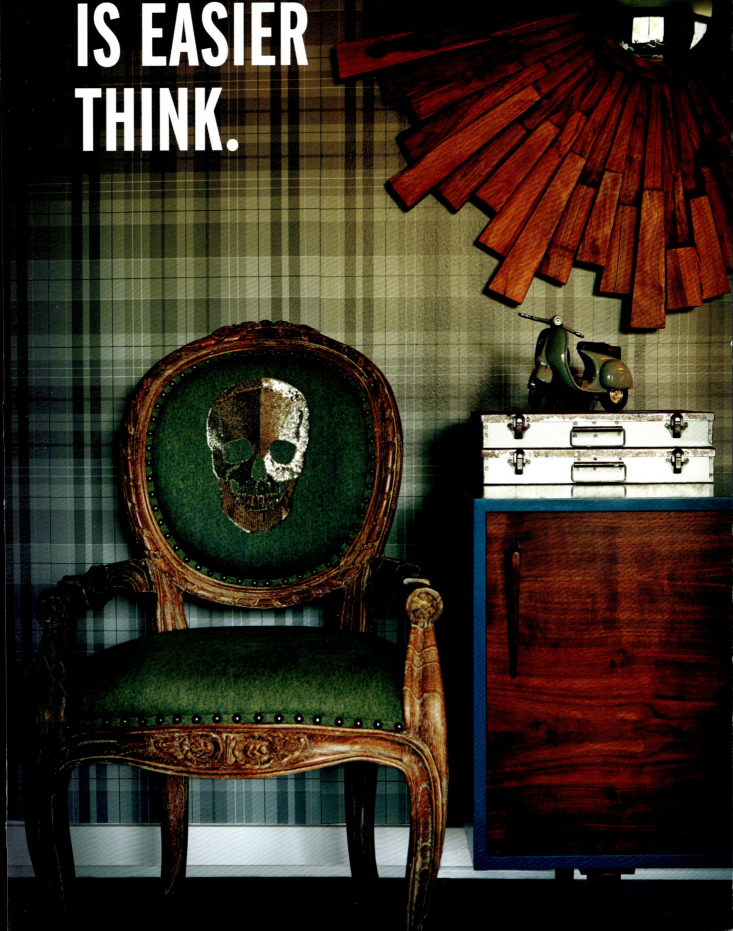

IS EASIER THINK.

60–30–10

I don't want you to get strung up with colour rules, but one formula I would recommend is the 60–30–10 rule. It's something I intuitively stick to.

When decorating a room, I'll start off by choosing one dominant colour to apply throughout, usually to floors, walls and ceiling. This is my **60** per cent: my unifying hue.

Next, I'll up the ante by adding into the mix a few hues that harmonise – my **30** per centers. I'm talking upholstery, and major pieces of furniture, in complementary colours.

Finally, I'll add my **10** per centers: the blingy accents. These guys take my scheme to new heights by adding sparkle and pizzazz. I might go glam and select golds and metallics (pages 66–9), or choose a few intoxicating contrasts.

You can have a zillion colours in a room, but to do this successfully you have to consider and vary the proportion of the pieces. Do that, and colour combining is a cinch!

The blast of grey in artist-designer Mariska Meijers' living room instantly makes the space feel edgy, whilst the harmonising hues of sofa and side table, and colour-popping accessories, elevate the whole look.

In my pad, I paint my walls dark and then ease in lighter colours through accessories, like my lamp and rug. It actually makes the space feel more spacious.

ONE FURTHER PIECE OF ADVICE: DON'T GET CAUGHT UP IN WHAT'S HOT OR WHAT'S NOT. SOMEONE ASKED ME RECENTLY WHAT HAPPENS WHEN BOTTOM-OF-THE-LAKE HUES ARE NO LONGER SEEN AS FASHIONABLE OR COOL. MY REPLY? I PAINTED MY HOUSE OUT IN DARK COLOURS WHEN IT WASN'T PERCEIVED AS TRENDY. I DON'T WORRY IF SOMETHING IS IN OR OUT. I JUST GO WITH WHAT I LOVE. AND IF I CROSS BACK OVER TO THE LIGHT SIDE, ASSUME I'VE BEEN TAKEN OVER BY ALIENS!

FANTА!

COLOUR

COMBOS

SING

COLOUR CAN

UPLIFT
INVIGORATE
SOOTHE
INTRIGUE

BASICALLY IT'S A MOOD-CHANGER. I THINK THAT ANY SPACE CAN TAKE ANY COLOUR. IT'S WHAT YOU DO WITH IT AND HOW YOU USE IT THAT WILL MAKE A SCHEME SUCCESSFUL OR NOT.

Bored of your kitchen? Do something unexpected and paint the inside of your cupboards an intoxicating red. Here the single red note stands in stark relief to the white walls. Love!

HERE ARE TEN OF MY FAVOURITE, UNEXPECTED COLOUR COMBINATIONS THAT TOTALLY WORK:

CHARTREUSE AND AQUA
ORANGE AND BLUE
INKY GREEN AND LIGHT PINK
PURPLE AND RED
PALE PINK AND RED-ORANGE
CHARCOAL AND MAGENTA
LAVENDER AND OLIVE
MINT GREEN AND TEAL
NAVY AND LILAC
CHARTREUSE AND LIME

(throw in a shot of pink and suddenly you're more chic than you ever imagined!)

BLACK AND WHITE

SUBVERT
EXPECTATIONS WITH
A FRESH TAKE ON A
CLASSIC COMBO.

Dramatic, elegant, and capable of making any room – from the bathroom to the kitchen – feel uber sophisticated, chic and timeless, you can't get more iconic than black and white.

Of course, clothes designers, from Chanel to Valentino, have understood this for years. Which is why I am forever pulling tear sheets from *Vogue* and other style mags, drilling down into high-fashion looks to get inspiration.

Be selective in how you use the two colours, and be ready to make a statement – this is a high-impact look. Once you start thinking out of the box, your space will feel fresher and more modern than the typical black floor, white wall scenario. My biggest tip would be to decide which of the hues you are going full-on with and then use the contrasting colour as the accent.

Balance is all-important, so vary the intensity and tones of the hues – introducing silvery greys, charcoals and milks – so that your scheme feels super intriguing. Metallics also bring this scheme alive. I use them all the time.

Being a fan of the inky palette, I lean a lot more heavily on the black side and only use white as an accent. So in my pad you'll find black walls, floors and ceilings, which I've punctuated with white dining chairs, blousy, fat-headed creamy hydrangeas, calico vases and so forth.

CLASSY, LUXE AND SUPER GLAM. AND THE BEST THING – IT'LL NEVER GO OUT OF FASHION!

Graphic and distinctive, the bold use of black and white in this bedroom – complete with chessboard print, Op Art stripes and patterns – makes for a fearless look that is anything but boring.

NO LONGER A MAINSTAY OF THE RUNWAYS, THIS PUNCHY PAIRING IS BIG ON THE HOME FRONT TOO.

Suave and sophisticated, the mash-up
of different materials in this bathroom
adds an unexpected dose of texture.

EVERYONE KNOWS THAT BLACK AND WHITE MAKE THE HOTTEST COUPLE EVER!

It's that balance between relaxing and invigorating that draws me to a black and white palette. That and the ease with which you can drop in other accent hues. This is demonstrated beautifully with the vibrant blue chair in Sarah Lavoine's elegantly monochrome, Parisian kitchen.

Unapologetic colour and pattern mix beautifully in artist-designer Mariska Meijer's Amsterdam abode. Note how the varying shades of just two colours – black and green – drive the scheme. A very clever colour technique!

BRIGHTS

AN INSTANT DASH OF ROCK 'N' ROLL.

Burnt orange, Barbie pink or neon orange, anyone? Rooms heavily punctuated with bold shots leap out at you.

But how do you use strong, intense hues successfully? Answer: decorate with confidence!

You need to believe in yourself to start dabbling with brights. But, trust me, any room can take bold gestures and a few shots of vivid. Even better if that room happens to be small because bold hues automatically make tiny spaces feel cooler and edgier than they really are. Clever that! It's a trick I use all the time. Bright hues distract the eye, so rather than noticing the size of a room, you only focus on how stylish it feels.

ADD SATURATED HUES
TO KNOCK YOUR PAD
OUT OF THE PARK.

Blue is such a powerful colour – dependable, strong, it feels luxurious and intoxicating at the very same time. It is used to brilliant effect opposite: the strong blue makes for a sophisticated statement wall; the white and neutrals tone the look down, creating a chilled-out effect.

I tend to use saturated hues in isolation, offsetting loud shades with plenty of neutrals, and using bright accessories – vases, cushions, over-dyed rugs – or jewel-toned upholstery, to pepper the room.

Integrating brightly patterned wallpaper or artwork, or colour-rich pillows into a scheme is an easy and intriguing way to make your interiors feel unique. Limiting the number of hues to two or three tones makes the brights look even more statement-worthy, and your room will still feel calm and laid-back. Then again, it's totally personal. If you want spaces to feel attention-grabbing and zippy, overdose on brights. Have confidence and experiment, I say!

EVERY SPACE NEEDS A
WAIT-A-MINUTE MOMENT:
MAKE BRIGHTS YOUR BFF!

SO RICH AND SO FABULOUS, AND PERFECT WHEN PARTNERED WITH LITERALLY ANY OTHER HUE.

I think the reason I am so obsessed with this palette is the mysterious mood these colours cast. Work with the spookiness and let corners and edges fade into darkness, as it adds far more drama and intrigue.

INKY HUES

This colour palette has been an obsession of mine for yonks. Why? Because anything you put against these bottom-of-the-lake greens, browns, greys and blacks looks and feels grander and edgier than it truly is. No one actually believes me on this until they try it (and then I receive the best emails!), but rather than making a room feel gloomy and depressing, inky hues give spaces an instant Hitchcockian vibe, and add oodles of interest.

Did you know that if a space faces north and receives little natural light, painting it out in a jolly hue or bright white won't transform a thing? Rather than fighting the problem, use it to your advantage. Make your space feel super-seductive, sophisticated and glamorous by painting it out in one of these dramatic, chalky, flat and deeply complex colours.

You can go so many different ways with a dark palette. Accent it with shiny, luminous metal accessories. I'm totally fixated on gold right now as it bounces the light around and looks and feels beautifully classic. So I have gold sconces on black walls; gold heads on mantles; little gold vases on tables. If that sounds too much, a pop of brights will give your space an instant exclamation mark. Even a mixture of textures will keep things interesting and avoid a one-note effect.

Don't shy away from the moodiness of this inky dark palette. You need to embrace shadows and let corners blur into darkness to give your space plenty of mystery. Done properly, these colours will change not only the way you think about your space but also the way you feel about it. My case rests!

BOTTOM-OF-THE-LAKE HUES TURN SPACES INTO ROOMS YOU WANT TO HUNKER DOWN IN AND NEVER LEAVE.

Painting a room out in a dark hue automatically makes it feel cosy, den-like and snug. No better place to do that than in the bedroom, I say!

Right: Dark, highly pigmented walls stand out against a vast expanse of window and a heavenly New York skyline. Athena Calderone's Brooklyn loft masters the balance between light and dark beautifully.

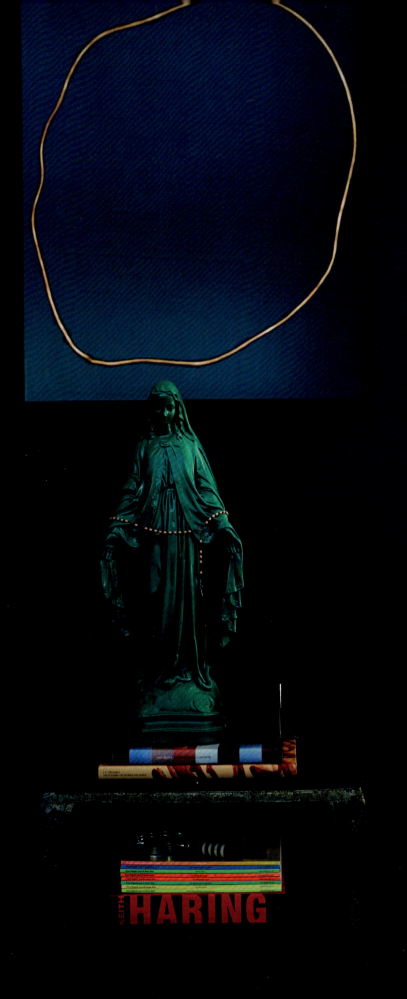

DARKER COLOURS EXAGGERATE COSINESS

Paint is the cheapest change you can make to any room and it's a game changer. Be warned that dark colours can look really bad when that first coat goes up, so don't quit after the first application. I know from heaps of experience that when the next coat goes up, magic happens. Paint out the trim, windows, floor, doorframes and ceiling in the same colour as the walls. When you blur the lines between walls and ceiling, the space automatically feels taller, grander, more sophisticated. You've created infinity!

Go for the flattest emulsion you can find for the walls: matte paint creates a luxurious, velvety effect. Go glossy on the ceiling; the light will bounce around beautifully, especially if you suspend a pendant or chandelier in the centre. To avoid small spaces feeling cramped, paint the odd bit of mismatched furniture in the same colour. Add a vibrant hue – wardrobe doors in teal, a small table in scarlet – to give your space a touch of unconventionality.

An inky palette with a shot of warm yellow is a marriage made in heaven. The yellow warms up the darker hue, adding a classy note.

DON'T
BE
AFRAID
OF
THE
DARK

NEUTRALS

EASY ON THE EYE
AND PERFECT FOR
COLOUR-PHOBES.

Neutral rooms don't have to be a bore. The trick is to create
contrast and avoid everything being too matchy-matchy.

Neutral colours are so warm, versatile and calming, they will
work anywhere and with any other hues. If everything is the
same tonality it can feel dull, so it's crucial to up the saturation
levels, and the contrast, to keep things fresh and crisp.

Imagine a room with strokes of taupe, khaki, rain-cloud
grey – beautiful simple hues. Undertones are important
here. So rather than white-on-white, select colours with soft
undertones of yellow, brown, violet even – where the palette
subtly changes with the light (see page 218).

Throw in some metallics, add oodles of different textures, a
dose of pattern, and you've nailed it!

The trick to decorating with neutrals is to create interest in the space through texture. Vary the shades of the neutrals and contrast the textures, as designer and artist Alina Preciado has done with her Brooklyn loft.

A mixture of sculptural furniture, unusual textures and organic surfaces creates the most beautiful dialogue. Although the milky alabaster/taupe/grey palette is quiet, the furniture in Kelly Wearstler's Malibu pad has a distinct personality. Unexpected and exciting.

NEUTRAL-RICH SPACES ARE SOPHISTICATED AND CHIC WHEN YOU OVERDOSE ON TEXTURE!

Mixing up materials can be just as exuberant as painting your pad out in vibrant hues. For a bit of theatre, get creative with texture. Designer Kyle Schuneman shows how it's done in his bold and beautiful West Hollywood pad.

THE NEUTRAL PALETTE

If you're thinking of sprucing up your walls with a fresh coat of paint, chances are you won't find anything on the shelves these days called plain old 'white'. Paint names have gone all fanciful, with brands preferring to evoke a lifestyle, emotion or story, rather than refer directly to the colour inside. (For more on the best paints in the market, turn to page 235).

THEN	V	NOW
BLUE		SLATE
BROWN		OTTER
CREAM		LAMBSKIN
GREEN		TURTLE
GREY		CLOUD
ICE BLUE		POLAR DRIFT
PALE GREY		GOING TO THE CHAPEL
PINK		NEWBORN
TAN		CAT'S PAW
TAUPE		KITTEN WHISKERS
WHITE		FALLING SNOW
YELLOW		BLONDE

Clever finishing touches, like this whimsical wallpaper, revitalise rooms. Who knew neutrals could be so glamorous?

THESE NEUTRAL, FOUNDATION COLOURS WORK ANYWHERE, ANYTIME.

METALLICS

I'M HAVING A LOVE AFFAIR WITH METALLICS; THESE GOLD DOORS TAKE THIS KITCHEN TO A WHOLE DIFFERENT LEVEL!

It's not often that my jaw hits the floor, but the soft gold kitchen cabinets in Jean-Louis Deniot's Parisian pad (opposite) left me speechless. To master the metallic look, bear in mind that there is a fine line between adding pieces that instantly brighten a room and going overboard so that your space begins to feel like a nightclub. Overdose on too many reflective surfaces, and it can feel overpowering. That said, when bling looks as beautiful as this, I'm hooked!

An elegant palette of white, grey and gold lends instant refinement to Jean-Louis Deniot's hallway. The look is further elevated by the combo of shiny and matte surfaces.

Right: A restrained neutral palette lends a sophisticated air to this bedroom. The sculptural piece of art shouts 'Ta Da!' while the quiet earthy palette adds a more sombre note. Perfect!

ALL THAT SHIMMERS IS BEAUTIFUL.

So how to get the balance just so? Probably the biggest tip I can give you is to avoid placing too many metallic pieces together. In my pad, for example, I have a little gold table next to a chair with a metallic leather cushion on it. The chair and the sheepskin draped over it tone the look down. Metallics can feel harsh and cold so it helps to offset them with softer elements: slubby wools, woods, velvet, pottery. Really layer on the texture.

Another trick is to put metallic accents near a window, as they help diffuse the light by bouncing it around.

I like to make a big impact with a few well-chosen pieces. So in my hallway, you'll find a supersized mirror, a gold oval table, and a shiny vase on the console – three statement pieces to glam up my look without overwhelming the scheme.

CHAMELEON *BROWN*

Brown is such a hardworking hue. You can use it as a bold statement or as an accent or sidekick. It's not one of those ballsy hues that shouts for attention, it just quietly, gently does its job, making it the perfect foundation on which to build any room.

Given my taste for the dark side, I gravitate towards slightly darker browns – the tones you would find in a gentleman's drinking club. But no matter which end of the spectrum you pull from, brown makes rooms feel instantly comfortable, grounded and safe.

For me, it's one of the most beautiful hues for living rooms as it encourages you to slow down, chill out and relax. I guess it's because it's the colour of the earth that it feels so immediately reassuring, but it's also weighty and robust.

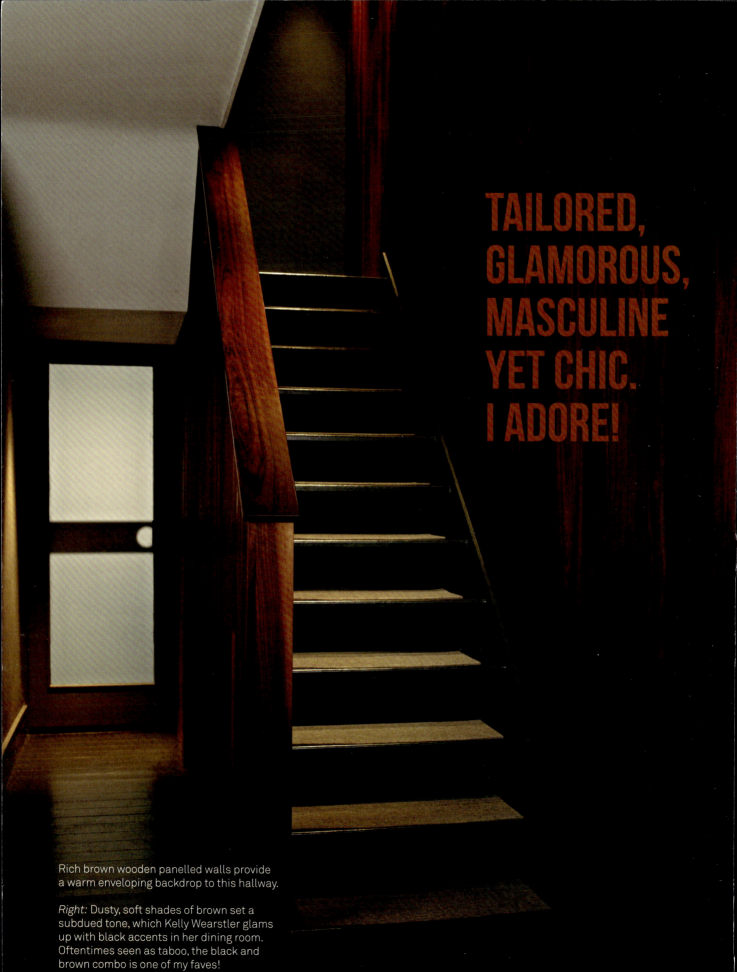

TAILORED, GLAMOROUS, MASCULINE YET CHIC. I ADORE!

Rich brown wooden panelled walls provide a warm enveloping backdrop to this hallway.

Right: Dusty, soft shades of brown set a subdued tone, which Kelly Wearstler glams up with black accents in her dining room. Oftentimes seen as taboo, the black and brown combo is one of my faves!

If you want your brown to have a bit more visual wallop, pair it with tangerine, powder blue or pearl grey. Nice! Dressing it up with stronger highlights, like acid yellows, lime green, or chartreuse, modernises it. Conversely, combining it with other neutrals tones it down. It's a chameleon this hue: timeless, durable and such an easy-on-the-eye colour to live with. Can you tell I'm its hugest fan?

PERFECT FOR CREATING A LOOK OF UNDERSTATED ELEGANCE

INTRIGUING SPACES

A successful colour scheme is one where harmony and continuity abound. But in order to take the space to the next level it has to be punctuated with a big dose of visual intrigue. The scheme opposite nails it!

At first sight, the library is thoroughly grounded in tradition with its 18th century family portrait hung on oak-panelled walls. What is so ingenious here is this knack for taking historical references and updating them in a sophisticated manner. For example, a pattern inspired by bark has been laser-printed onto canvas, abutting the oak walls. Suddenly you're creating this intriguing form of provocation by juxtaposing something very classical (oak) with something incredibly contemporary (canvas wallpaper), but in a super subtle way.

The scheme is held together and grounded by beautiful browns and neutrals, but the mix of cutting-edge pieces, classical references and subtle patterns results in an alluring signature style of low-key luxe. Genius!

BUILDING
SPACE

A THROUGH COLOUR

GOING FOR BOLD

It's much more interesting to play with colour than to play it safe. Matching is out. Bright pops of colour are in. They make you grin with delight, add drama and movement, and (believe it or not) mix beautifully with their neutral counterparts. When you add vivid intoxicating hues like sizzling orange, vibrant green or deep blue, you'll find that they will actually make you want to linger longer in a space. Promise!

1. Paint a wall in a colour that scares you, for some high impact, visual intrigue. It's only a wall and you can paint it back in an hour if you hate it!

2. Add a dash of bold by bringing in one, brightly coloured accessory or piece of furniture. Introducing hues in this way is much easier and it will boost your confidence when it comes to making bigger decorating decisions.

3. Take it slowly. Halls, bathrooms or guest bedrooms are typically small and great places to experiment if you're feeling a bit hesitant.

4. Restrict the number of hues to around three. You don't need much: just a punch to give the space an exclamation mark!

5. Colours in a space should flow, so if you're going to paint your kitchen units red, make sure you add touches of red in the accessories to make the room feel balanced.

UP THE SATURATION LEVEL!

Rooms heavily punctuated with intense colours leap out at you; the results are creative, inviting and unapologetically glam. I think that any room can take some bold gestures and a few shots of vivid, no matter how big or how small. Spaces that pop automatically feel edgier and cooler than they really are. Clever colour!

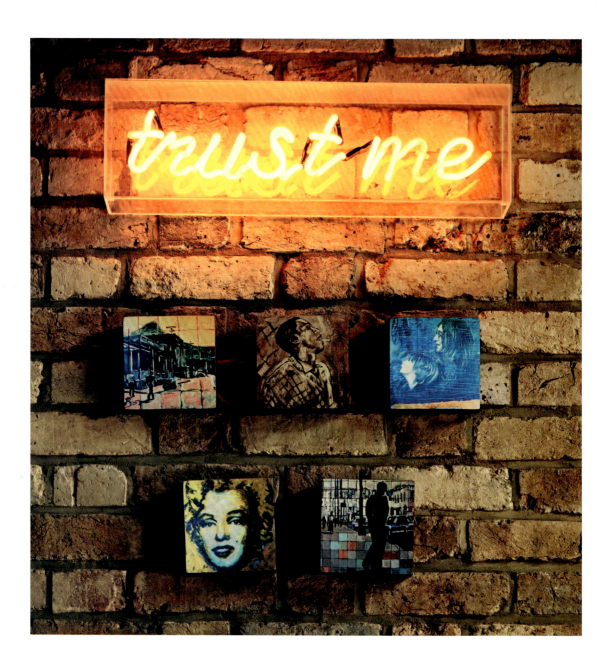

NEON

Neon is a fab way of bringing vibrancy and a jolt of colour to your pad without going overboard. Sue Miller shows how it's done (above) with a pop of yellow neon writing creating an instant exclamation mark on her kitchen wall. You can integrate neon decor into anything from artwork to tables, lighting to accessories. But it can be hard to get right. For maximum impact and sophistication, I reckon it looks best in isolated pops. Just be careful is all I'm saying!

MAKE A PLAIN TABLE
POP: THINK PINK LEGS
& COLOURFUL BOOKS.

TEXTURE

Texture makes rooms more interesting. It creates ambience. And the best thing is, you can never overdose on it! The trick is to cause friction and put as many different materials in a room as possible. I'm talking hand-tufted rugs, oodles of sofa cushions, gilded frames, wooden tables, hand-thrown vases, wicker...

If you gravitate towards feminine interiors, then lots of soft fine fabrics, smooth woods and shiny accessories will do the job nicely. If you're more attracted to the masculine feel (c'est moi), then a combo of rustic metals, rich woods and velvet sofas works a treat.

Texture doesn't have the pulling power of pattern or colour. Your eye will not automatically dart to it, so you really need to pile on those contrasts. It's the 'opposites attract' approach: pit rough against smooth, super glossy against nubby, coarse against fine, modern against trad. Mix up your accessories – avoid everything being super glam or rustic, it can feel a little one-dimensional.

Right: The more you rein in the colour palette, the more you can go to town with texture. Case in point: zigzag rug, leather chair and plaid wallpaper!

WITH A REINED-IN
COLOUR PALETTE, YOU
CAN REALLY PILE ON
THE CONTRASTS WITH
PATTERN AND TEXTURE.

Luxurious yet tactile, this Parisian bedroom cum home office (designed by Elodie Sire) is a space I want to move into right now!

YOU CAN CREATE TEXTURE IN SO MANY WAYS.

Lighting is a game changer: with enough lights to add little pools of radiance around the room, you can introduce depth, texture, character and ambience (see pages 104–7).

Flowers and plants add another subtle layer (pages 118-22), as do accessories. Rugs define a space and cosy things up. Again you're aiming for maximum contrast, so on smoothly skimmed concrete floors I've got slubby Moroccan rugs rather than flat weaves. Mix up your soft furnishings, too. Let's say you have a woollen cushion on your sofa, well instead of going for more wool (so boring!), introduce a completely new texture, like leather, velvet or silk. It's the interplay of different materials – grainy chenille cushions with velvet blankets, thick wool with thin muslin – that brings spaces alive.

My bedroom with its warm enveloping velvety walls, softened with a vintage Moroccan rug, a merino throw and a sheepskin. Luxe and squishy, it's a place I rarely want to leave!

MIND THE GAP

Want to decorate like a pro? The big trick is to make whatever you're styling feel like it's always been there.

Paintings, mirrors and wall sconces turn flat surfaces into something more intriguing.

When it comes to styling mantelpieces, shelves and consoles, steer away from stuffy and over-considered, and think laidback lair.

Prop up your art for that cool bohemian vibe. Up the verticals. By which I mean, elongate the space by displaying something tall, like picture frames, flowers or plants. No matter how high or low your ceilings, it ups the impact.

Mirrors are great. The more oversized you make them, the grander, edgier and cooler your room will look!

A trio of objects always works; whether you're arranging accessories, pillows, flowers, just follow the Rule of Three!

The components to this home office are minimal, yet everything feels luxurious thanks to fabric clad walls and a supersized mirror, which gives the illusion of a much grander space.

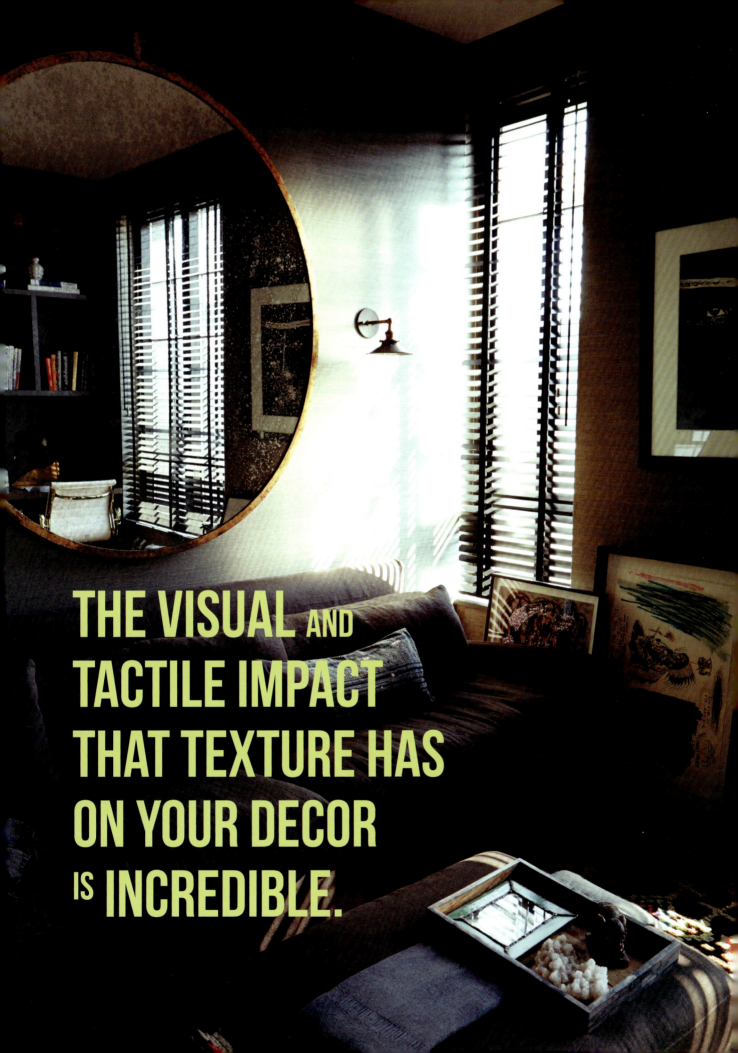

THE VISUAL AND TACTILE IMPACT THAT TEXTURE HAS ON YOUR DECOR IS INCREDIBLE.

STATEMENT PAINT

There's a big trend towards using paint not just as a backdrop but also as a decorative tool, and a way to make a statement.

Gloss is being used for striking effect, as it gives spaces such a contemporary vibe (see page 226). Take it one step further and paint an accent wall out in gloss and the rest in matte, using the same hue. Matte finishes are calm and serene, gloss finishes are high energy and exciting, and it's that friction between the two that creates the magic.

I've seen a shift recently away from 'effects' and towards high-end paints with a chemical make-up and an intense (highly saturated) hue. So rather than dragging, rolling or stippling, it's now all about contrasting finishes, whether you are mixing and matching colour families or using more of a holistic palette.

Something I've often done for clients is to paint the ceiling out in a glossy hue, with the walls painted in the same hue, in matte. This works beautifully in dining rooms if you happen to suspend a chandelier below: as the light glimmers, it looks spectacular.

If you fancy going super-glam, consider lacquering a wall. In which case, it's best to spray the paint as it has to be applied totally smoothly and requires multiple coats (at least four or five). Or how about painting a stripe of gloss on a matte wall? It's not as time-consuming as doing a whole lacquer, but produces a nice, subtle finish. Super chic!

You could opt for a metallic paint: perfect for a high-impact decorative finish and your pad will sparkle once you're done. Or look into clay paints with faux finishes, which mimic European plaster. By this I mean the painted walls take on a subtle almost fabric-like texture with the paint being the consistency of yogurt. Love!

PATTERN

Pattern is a fundamental part of design, adding depth and visual kudos as well as texture, diversity and colour.

Now, I happen to know from experience that many people are scared of introducing and piling on pattern – and when I say pattern I mean anything striped, flowered, checked, graphic or geometric. Certainly, if you want your space to look and feel cohesive, you do need to be smart when it comes to mixing things up.

But, fear not. If you're new to the pattern game, it's easy to start small. Accessories and textiles are the simplest route to go down, so add a couple of contrasting patterned cushions, decorative vases or rugs (see pages 96–7), and see the dimensions of your room change before your eyes.

The more you rein in the colour palette, the more you can mix pattern to your heart's content. If you don't believe me, check out Mariska Meijers' Amsterdam home (opposite). Patterned walls, patterned rug. Tantalising!!

The shades in the patterns you opt for will have a big impact on your space, so pay attention to colour combinations. High voltage contrasts create an energetic feeling whilst subtler hues will contribute to a calmer, more subdued environment

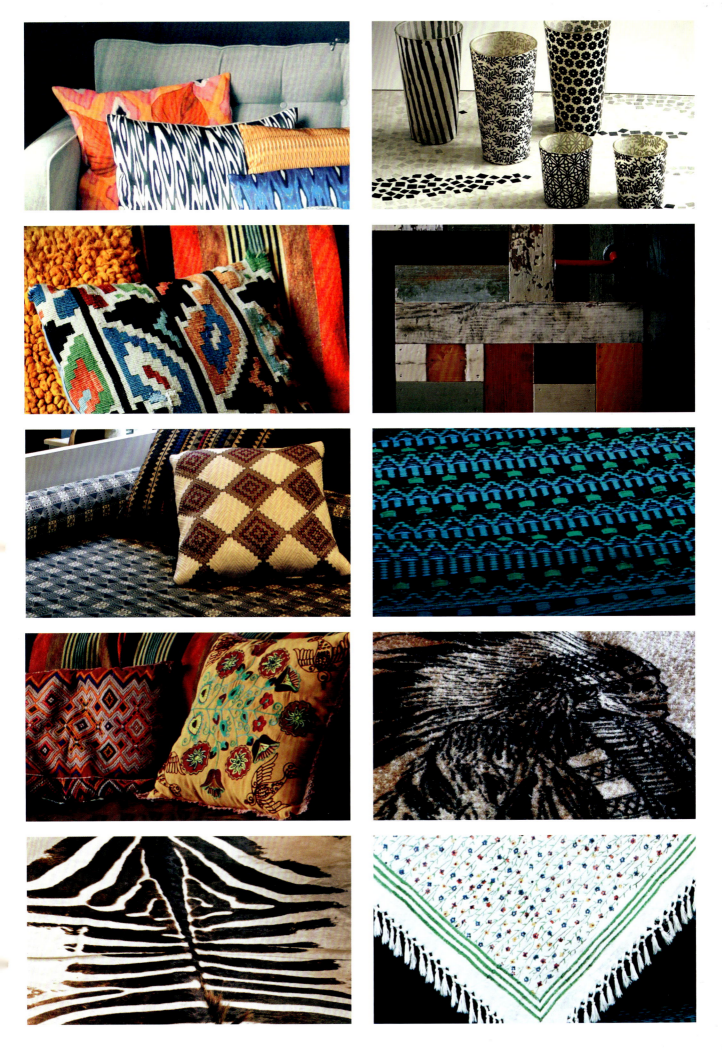

MAKE A SUBTLE PALETTE EDGY

The tamer the hues, the wilder you can go with pattern. On my lower ground floor at home, I have a ton of rugs skimming the concrete, with different motifs from various sources all over the globe, but because the palette is homogeneous they blend beautifully.

Add friction by varying the scale. Lots of small-scale patterns in a room can result in a one-way ticket to Dullsville, so mix it up a tad. The more you vary the scale, the more you confuse the eye so it doesn't know where to focus (exactly our plan!). The more we confuse the eye, the more intriguing a room becomes.

Avoid anything too co-ordinated and matchy matchy. I've achieved my best results from simply experimenting with contrasting patterns – pairing say skinny stripes with out-of-proportion flowers, for example.

You don't have to have a grand plan when it comes to introducing pattern – a dash of spontaneity is a good thing. So if you like it, go for it!

NATURAL LIGHT

The thing about decorating with natural light is not to get too hung up about whether your pad receives dim, indirect northern light or bright southern beams. It's actually how you utilise the light that counts.

On my side of the pond, rooms with a northern exposure receive indirect light. These rooms are actually my favourite kind – artists love them too – because the light remains pretty consistent, with fewer shadows and less contrast. To avoid north-facing spaces feeling depressing, the trick is to throw in a few shimmery surfaces and metallics, so that the light can bounce around. You can paint your walls any colour, no matter where your house faces (every other book you'll read on the subject will tell you otherwise, but trust me on this!). I have successfully painted north-facing rooms in cool tones and they've looked and felt amazing because I've accented with warmer tones. Accent hues turn rooms around, so think about accessorising with shots of pink, coral, saffron, yellow, burnt orange. Happy hues!

- At home, I've removed all the internal doors, except for those on bedrooms and bathrooms, to allow the natural light to flow through. It's so transformative!

- I'm not a fan of bulky window treatments, so no heavy curtains or ornate pelmets for us. Shutters, and simple blinds will help you optimise the daylight.

- The more shiny surfaces you can add to a room, the lighter that room will feel – so overdose on sparkly chandeliers, gold knobs, silver photo frames and candlesticks.

- Add mirrors, especially if your space is particularly light-deprived. A mirror will reflect natural light and create the illusion of a larger space. In fact, it has the capacity to double the light in a room. Super-size the mirror and you will capture even more light!

Work your windows. Choose treatments that maximise natural light. Roller blinds work beautifully in this bathroom, adding an air of serentiy that is enhanced by the neutral colour palette.

Opposite: Natural light positively effects mood, so if you are lucky enough to have large windows, utilise them to the max, and dress sparingly.

South-facing rooms are brighter, which is why so many people paint them out in cool blues or refreshing greens to soften the look. Don't worry about doing the same; just make sure you accent with some lovely tones. I plump for oodles of caramel and mocha, with a few shots of lime, maybe.

Whether your rooms face north, east, west or south, I'd recommend a plethora of warm and cool tones in each, because I actually like the friction it creates. As I am forever banging on about, the more friction you create in a space, the more interesting it will feel.

Short of knocking down walls, building an entire wall of windows or adding skylights, there isn't much you can do to increase the natural light in your home. Instead, work with what you've got and either maximise it to the full or tone it down.

LIGHTING

Like me in my early days, I find that most people devote
a lot of time and thought to colours, furniture, styles and
materials, but then sort of forget about the lighting. In fact,
I would say that this is probably the single, most common
mistake I see, time and time again.

But lighting is instrumental in a room's transformation –
enhancing colours, adding depth and drama, and creating
a mood. Truly, it has magical powers: highlighting, drawing
the eye in, making a space look bigger, cosier, you name it.

Theatrical, dramatic and clad
in scene-stealing gold, I don't
think I've seen a more beautiful
table lamp!

THE BIG THREE

When we light spaces we never want to over light them, as shadows create mystery and drama. In order to achieve this effect, there are three categories of interior lighting you need to know about: ambient (or general), task, and accent. A successful lighting scheme requires a combo of all three; it's what we in the biz call 'layering'.

1.

First up, **ambient lighting**: this provides general illumination and is most often found in recessed lighting, chandeliers and other ceiling fixtures. Recessed halogens, positioned around the perimeter of a room, can fool the eye by appearing to push back the walls.

But go easy on the down lights: avoid zillions in each and every ceiling, so that rooms are lit up like an airport runway. Dimmers are key here, as they will enable you to control the amount of illumination according to the daylight. You'll get far more control over brightness and mood with dimmers, so as the day progresses you can control various lighting scenes.

2.

Task is concentrated lighting for performing certain tasks – writing, reading, cooking – and will create those intriguing shadows we love. Sit down on any chair in my pad and you'll find a small table next to it with a table lamp, perfect for casting a warm atmospheric glow.

3.

Task lighting on its own creates too much contrast. So you need to layer this with **accent lighting** (my favourite!). I'm talking candlelight, decorative sconces or picture lights that highlight things: artwork, architecture, textiles, groups of vases, you name it. You can't work or read with accent lighting; it is solely about creating atmosphere. In my pad, as dusk falls, I go from a space lit mostly by daylight to an atmospheric intimate zone – which feels immediately snug and cosy. Layered and theatrical, it beckons me in.

Above: I am a big fan of classic task lights like this one. They provide the perfect amount of light, never date, and bring areas alive. Clever, no?

Below: Aside from being practical, lamps should catch the eye, adding whimsy, charm and drama to any living space.

Opposite: There are so many ways to go with chandeliers: bold, blingy, retro, rustic. No matter which, adding one to any space provides instant razzle dazzle, as seen in this hallway.

HANG PENDANTS OR CHANDELIERS MUCH LOWER THAN YOU THINK YOU SHOULD.

A row of three pendants takes centre stage here, giving the room an artful touch. The lower you can hang pendants, the taller the room will appear. Plus those extra inches will change the vibe of a dining area, making it feel instantly cooler and more atmospheric.

FURNITURE

When it comes to furniture, nobody wants to change up the big pieces in a hurry, so I like to take my time when it comes to figuring out what colour profile I'm after. Go with pieces you are completely head-over-heels in love with and a common theme usually emerges. One of my favourite tricks is to knock back the colour on the big pieces – sofas, beds, dining tables – and opt for more daring hues on smaller items, so you can swap in and swap out should you get bored.

Accent chairs are a great way of adding pops of colour and a touch of whimsy to your space. I have them all over my pad. You can use them as space fillers, as conversational nooks next to a fireplace or beside the window; in hallways, bedrooms, studies, even plopped under trees in the garden! Whether you plump for armchairs, ottomans, benches or recliners, the trick is to ensure the chair has some point of difference – a bold colour, pattern or texture: something that makes it stand out.

Don't worry about practicality; accent chairs don't need to be super comfortable or even functional. I've got a rocking chair made out of concrete, and a chair in the kitchen that is broken so you can't actually sit on it, but I love its form and it enlivens the area it's in.

Add intrigue by counterbalancing statement furniture with other attention grabbing pieces, so your room feels complex and intriguing (see pages 182–91).

Upholstered pieces are the anchor of any living room. The more loungey you go, the more sumptuous your space. Incidentally the pendant was inspired by seaweed – apt for a home overhanging the Pacific Ocean!

A BRIGHT SHOWSTOPPER BENCH: PERFECT AS A PERCH, PERFECT FOR HOUSING STUFF.

I am a little obsessed with X-benches, particularly this blue tufted velvet one in Athena Calderone's Brooklyn pad. Perfect as a perch, but also alone, anchoring the painting, it makes an instant statement.

Mirrors are one of the most important elements in turning a room around, and just as statement-worthy as a bigger piece of furniture. I would love to encourage you to supersize them. They're your best friends when it comes to expanding horizons and adding intrigue to any space you put them in. A super important decorating tool, too – nothing else adds such instant grandeur!

Another game changer are little tables. Tucked or nestled by armchairs or sofas, or placed at the end of a bed or in a hallway, little tables help soften a room but at the same time give it vitality. Anywhere there is a chair or a sofa in my house, you'll find a table.

Oddly enough, I fashion all sorts of things into tables, from African drums to apple crates, stools, even poufs, so don't feel you have to go down the conventional route. Ignore all that mumbo jumbo about heights and dimensions. The more you ditch the rules, the more intriguing a room becomes.

One more thing: if you can, opt for circular tables. They will transform your room, breaking up all those rigid, straight lines. I love breaking rooms down and figuring out what makes them work. However flat your current scheme, with a bit of poking around and digging deep, you'll find a formula before too long!

Whether it's a dining table or a coffee table in your living room, tables are the heart and soul of a room. These high shine glass ones look more regal when barely decorated.

Trebling up three small coffee tables to look like one is genius to my mind.

Right: A pair of 1960s Knoll sofas are coupled with a cocktail table and parchment side tables housing a lamp from the Sixties. Using the subtlest of palettes, it's a look that shouts luxe!

GREENERY

It doesn't matter what other colours are going on in your pad, greenery refreshes and invigorates areas of your home like nothing else. The trick is to look at plants or flowers in the same way as you would any other accessory. Think about their shape, their colour, their texture – and, above all, play about with scale.

Many plants resemble amazing sculptures, adding bundles of liveliness to any shelf, mantle or console. To add a subtle layer of texture and dimension, the trick, as always, is to mix it up. If you pot everything in round, shiny pots, the effect is a big yawn. So mix pointy plants with feathery; small with large; matte with shiny containers; round with square; wicker with concrete. You might have a plant with glossy leaves on one table, ferns on another. You might have fat-headed peonies sitting next to dainty cornflowers. It's the contrast that brings rooms alive!

I like to create little still lifes with plants, so, for example, I'll gather a whole host of succulents (which look super sweet) and create a mini installation. This is a go-to trick I use for every accessory actually. When you group things, as opposed to leaving gaps, your eye takes in the whole and the effect is far more impactful.

The easiest way to bring the outdoors in is to accessorise with indoor plants. The more you mix up their textures, the cooler the display.

ENTRYWAYS

Hallways or entryways tend to be one of the most neglected spaces in our homes. They are such transitional areas, we are forever whizzing in and zooming out of them. However, when I come home at night after an exhausting day, I want to walk through the door and be enveloped by a feeling of squishy contentment. And the only way you achieve that is for your entryway to create a strong first impression.

Colour plays an integral part here, because your hallway sets the style for what is to come. I would like to challenge you to think about these spaces differently and decorate them as you would your living room. I can almost bet you have some intoxicating, colourful artwork or accessories in your living room, so why not here? Turn your entryway into a space filled with colour, lamps, books, flowers, nik naks – all the stuff that will transport you to a magical, relaxed place.

Be more daring. The great thing about entryways is that they are generally the smallest area to revamp, and are only used as walkthroughs, so take risks, as it will not be such a chore to start again. In my hallway, I actually want people to stop and linger longer, hence darkly painted red-black walls, a gold table, and a few giant-size faux cactus plonked by the front door. Nailed!

Use colour as your jumping-off point and it's an instant game changer. These are not the easiest spaces to make homely or stylish – often narrow, with long stretches of uninterrupted hall – so it really helps to start mixing your hues, harmonising some, jarring others. It gets a little addictive, just to warn!

Faux walls that look like marble (but are actually achieved with a paint effect) make Jean-Louis Deniot's entryway one of the coolest of all time. Even cleverer, behind the painting is a secret door leading into the kitchen. J'adore!

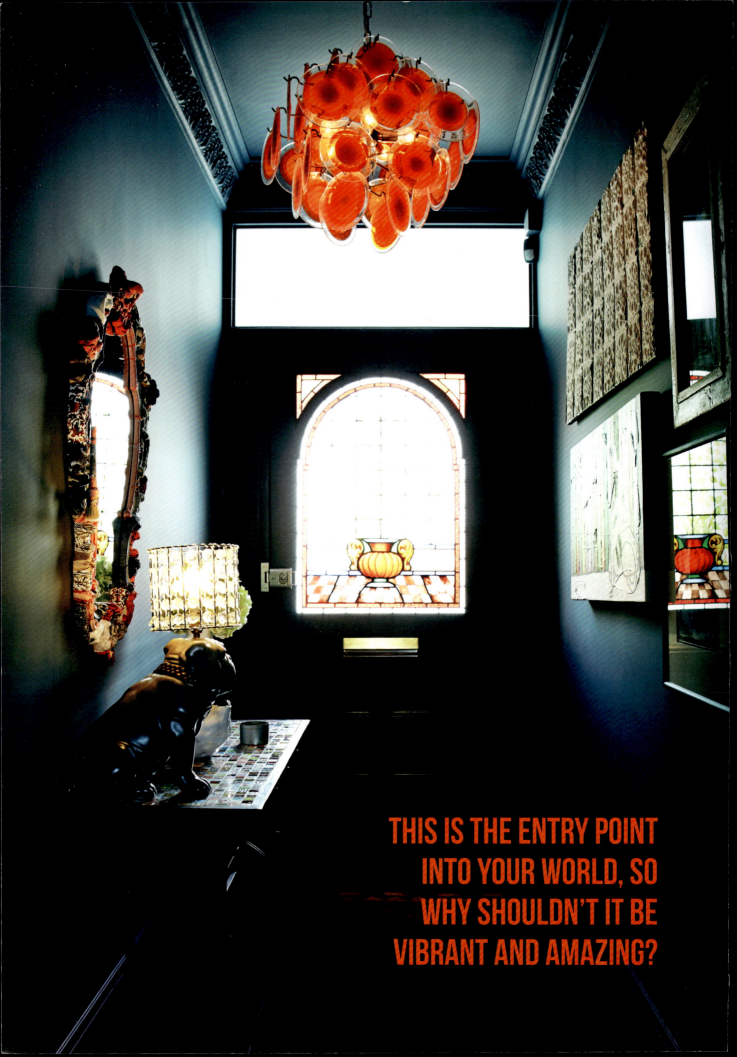

THIS IS THE ENTRY POINT INTO YOUR WORLD, SO WHY SHOULDN'T IT BE VIBRANT AND AMAZING?

The offbeat combination of art in this entryway gives the space serious charisma. If you have a relaxed sensibility, the more you don't match, the cooler your space can be!

Opposite: If you decorate your hallway like your living room, you'll suddenly find that you want to linger longer, as I do in Sue Miller's London entranceway. Add art, mirrors wrapped in fabric, and a quirky dog light, and you've got it nailed!

No matter if your hallway is super skinny or grand, think outside of your comfort zone when it comes to decorating. Any sort of table or console (no matter how skinny) or storage unit works a treat for storing hats, gloves, bags, keys – all the messy stuff. Then you can go two ways: 1. Blend the furniture into the wall colour or 2. Make it pop with something uber punchy.

Pattern is important, too. The biggest trick here is to fool the eye away from the potential awkwardness of this space. A patterned rug skimming the floor, or a runner, up the stair treads, will give your hallway instant pizzazz (and not show the dirt). The bolder the better I say.

Glam, decorative and cool, this walk-through hallway uses natural accents to ensure a beautiful flow from one space to the other. Each room is decorated differently, but the consistency of the palette holds the look together.

If your hallway is small or oddly shaped, hanging artwork 'salon style' will elevate it to new heights. You'll take the attention away from its shape, and towards how cool it is. Plus artwork is a great place to start if you're a little worried about colour.

Don't neglect the finishing touches in hallways. Mirrors will reflect light, both natural and artificial, and instantly double the impression of your space. And you can soften the decor with the soft orange glow of a lamp or some seasonal blooms – from hydrangeas in deepest blue in summer, to intoxicating, blackberry-red roses in winter – greeting you with a blast of colour every time you enter.

You pass through this space so many times a day, why not make it as beautiful as possible. Rooms devoid of pieces lack intrigue, so in order to create a space that causes the heart to skip a beat you have to introduce colour and decoration. It's as simple as that!

TRANSITIONING

When you wander from room to room, no matter if you live in a small apartment or a palace, it's important to consider how your colour palette flows through the space and how everything sits together. I plump for a continuous harmonious flow and add elements of surprise through accessories rather than paint colour. But you might not want things to flow. So you could opt for a dark hallway and a light living room.

THERE IS NO WRONG OR RIGHT. IT'S COMPLETELY PERSONAL!

KITCHENS

I am obsessed with cooking. I read recipe books at night like novels, and go to farmers' markets weekly. In fact, most Saturday mornings you'll find me at either our local farmers' market or at Monmouth in Borough, drinking coffee at 7.30 a.m. with the two Ms. Kid you not!

All of this means, of course, that I love my kitchen. I spend a lot of time in mine – it's a way of unwinding at the end of the day or over the weekend.

Kitchens are tough to get right because they have to be supremely practical. But, particularly if yours is open plan, like mine, it is vital to embellish and add to this space or it will feel disconnected from the rest of your pad.

Many people shy away from colour in the kitchen, opting instead for a subdued palette of creams, granite greys and browns. But an unexpected hue will elevate this space like nothing else. I wanted my kitchen to feel glam, with a boho edge, so I went for colours that are deep and sophisticated.

If you're feeling confident, you could take the plunge and paint the whole kitchen in an intoxicating hue, or paint out the units. It will give your kitchen an instant face-lift! Otherwise limit yourself to just one wall, a brightly coloured backsplash or just a handful of small accessories: funky coloured bar stools or a few bright vases, sculptures and platters can bring in lovely splashes of colour.

A SPLASH OF COLOUR IS YOUR VITAL INGREDIENT HERE!

I adore the time-worn look of this old, old butcher's block island, coupled with the industrial architecture. Cosy, calm and soothing, especially offset against the dark wall. It's knocked further out of the park by Alina Preciado's finishing touches.

I've come across some colour combos that have made these spaces look stunning – colours that you would never think to put together, let alone in a kitchen: brights mixed with lights, cool colours with warm, even two shades of the same hue butting up against each other. How about red and bright pink – these hues look incredible together. Turquoise and tangerine? Cobalt blue and fuchsia? Violet and marigold?

The more you can accessorise your kitchen, the more integrated it will feel. One of the biggest tips I can give you is to pile stuff in there that you wouldn't normally think of. Not just rugs, but paintings, a spare chair, chandeliers – pieces that you would normally put in your living rooms. On my kitchen island I always have a massive bowl of apples (we are obsessed with juicing at AA HQ), plus I've plonked the hugest faux fig on the counter to play around with scale.

Another game-changing tip is to add some open-plan storage, because if everything is behind closed doors the room will feel boring. However, throw in an open plan unit or shelves, accessorise with some storage jars, recipes books, linens, colourful platters and so on, and suddenly you've elevated your space to a whole other level without really doing that much.

A chalkboard wall sets a fun tone in the kitchen.

Left: Subtle hues of dusty rose
and grey are a magical combo
is this tiny kitchen, designed by
Elodie Sire. Even more genius, the
furniture hasn't been downsized to
fit in with the small space.

The reined-in colour palette
makes this kitchen feel bigger
than it really is. Clever!

White on white doesn't get boring in this marble kitchen (by Kelly Wearstler), as the subtle variation in hue and pattern animates the space.

BATHROOMS

Imagine dark walls, beautiful gold fixtures, a space you will never want to leave.

Whether it is through colour, wallpaper, tiles, accessories, pattern, texture or all of the above, bathrooms that take risks are the ones that stand out from the crowd, thanks to that element of the unexpected. In mine you'll find a supersized chandelier, a rug, a chair, art even.

PAINT

I say it a zillion times a day, but the most transformative thing you can do to any room is change the paint colour. Forget safe, wishy-washy pale walls, I want you to paint in a ground-breaking, daring-to-be-different way. As odd as it sounds, many dark colours have the hugest amount of warmth in them, which soften and cocoon the room – exactly what you need at the end of the day or the beginning of a new one, for that matter. Or imagine hits of bright colour, delivered through vases or artwork, a glam shower curtain or a rug that takes your breath away.

FIXTURES

I am a fan of gold, not *a la* Donald Trump, splashed everywhere, but gold fixtures in isolation are beautiful. Warmer and sexier than their stainless- or brushed-chrome counterparts, they look fabulous in bathrooms. You can opt for bright and shiny, or polished and soft. This look has even filtered down to the high street. I brought the sweetest little sink with gold taps from B&Q recently for a song – £60 and I love it!

An ornate supersized mirror injects instant personality into this bathroom.

Marble, marble everywhere – from the sink
to the walls, to the floor! Opulent, luxurious
and enhanced further by this magical
palette of greys and greens.

Right: How bold should you go in a
bathroom? This bold, I say! A bathroom
drenched in floor-to-ceiling marble makes
for a major, dizzying statement.

A serene and calm bathroom is given a jolt with the black bath. Further black accents move the space out of bland territory into wow territory.

WALLPAPER

Forget all that mumbo jumbo about not being able to paper bathrooms; you absolutely can. In the past there was a problem with humidity, but now bathrooms are ventilated well and almost all papers work. Wallpaper is an amazing enhancement to a bathroom, because it is so unexpected. What is even more exciting is the choice out there. You can go down the architectural route – tin tiles, concrete, wooden panels – or you can go down a pattern route or a colourful route. Almost anything goes.

FURNITURE

Storage is key and fundamental for hiding lotions, potions and all the rest of the stuff that is unattractive to have out on display. Vanities that are wall-hung look super sleek, or go floor to ceiling and paint out the same colour as your walls; the storage unit will disappear.

Add an accent chair or an occasional table to take away the utilitarian feel of the bathroom and turn it into more of a laidback lair, perfect for relaxing, hanging out in and generally winding down.

ACCESSORIES

Bathrooms should reflect the rest of your space, so that when you walk into them you won't just find the loo, the sink and the tub. Under-accessorised, I find them a little 'Plain Jane'. But once you start adding layers, candles, art, rugs, stools, plants and sculptures, you completely change the vibe of the space and cosy it up.

Rethink the bland and boring, choose a paint colour that sings to you, and you'll start living in a magical world, from which there is no return, as everything else feels not good enough.

PROMISE, PROMISE, PROMISE!

LIVING ROOMS

I don't know about you guys, but my living room does a lot of double dutying. It's the media room, somewhere to chill watching a late-night movie, eating take-out pizza from the box (half of it goes to the two Ms). It's the impromptu office – you'll find me on the sofa gone seven, answering that constant stream of emails. And it's my contemplation area, where I'll pause, stretch full-out and just listen to the fire gently crackling away – my favourite thing to do, ever!

I became a bit obsessed actually, trying to figure out the trick for creating a multi-functional living space that automatically feels vibrant but also relaxing. A living room that you want to hang out in, hunker down in, use to chill out or entertain. I want mine to feel supremely glam for those Friday night soirées, where Old Fashioneds come at you thick and fast!

Keeping everything (chairs, coffee table and accessories) low draws the eye horizontally, which feels just right in relation to the window. These close-to-the-floor pieces signal casual, on-the-floor hanging out.

THE BEST LIVING ROOMS PLAY
WITH COLOUR, BUT DON'T OVERDO IT.

When you match in duos, you can mix your furniture styles far more easily, seen here in this beautiful arrangement from Alina Preciado's home.

Pattern brings the dark hues in this
living area alive. It feels edgy, decadent
and perfect for a small space!

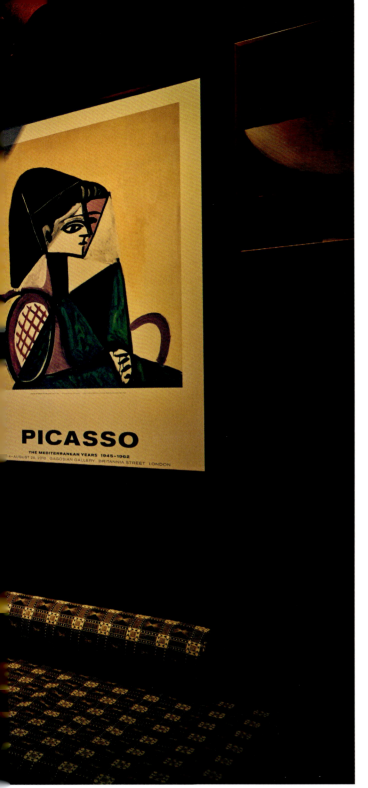

Is there a formula for creating that fairy dust magic that makes living rooms feel aspirational, inspirational, creative, yet laid back? The good news is YES there is. And guess what, it's colour!

All amazing living rooms play with colour but don't overdo it. There is such a fine line between creating spaces that feel too bland and ones that feel crazy. The trick is to restrict the colour palate. The homes pictured here might use a lot of intoxicating hues, but you'll never find more than three or four going on in the same room.

Add a hue that gives your space a touch of unconventionality. Who wants a living room that follows the crowd? Maybe you could paint a side table out in scarlet red, or treat an alcove in a vibrant blue or even go the whole hog and paint the entire space black. I have! These intoxicating hues (off-radar notes, as I like to call them) turn spaces around. I'm talking saffron; magenta; peacock; inky, swampy green. Scared? Don't be. Colours like this take spaces to new levels and you can accent with them in small touches – a vase, a lamp base, a piece of art – to update your look.

Not everything has to be colourful. I am the biggest fan of neutrals and chameleon browns – I use them more than brights – as they won't fight for attention like your more colourful finds. But they will give your wow pieces breathing space. I'm also obsessed with adding vintage pieces to my space – tables, consoles, an ornately carved mirror: items that tell a narrative and have a patina no matter how subtle.

I am a big fan of rugs in living rooms. The pile is super important – the thicker and fluffier the better. Don't go for one solid hue. Opt instead for rugs with a pattern, no matter how small the motif. It will make the space feel far more interesting. Remember to overdose on texture (it cosies the space up), so juxtapose rough with smooth, shiny with hand woven.

In a nutshell, living rooms that reach for the next level marry together intoxicating and toned-down hues, mix vintage with modern, timeless with quirky, and overdose on texture. Multi-dazzling combos, and the more you push them, the more tantalising the vibe!

ADD MORE THAN ONE FOCAL POINT, SO THE EYE IS EXCITED & ENGAGED WHEREVER IT LOOKS.

A disciplined colour palette (mostly dominated by browns) is accentuated and enhanced by the graphic drama of patterned cushions and rugs. The eclectic selection of furniture makes the space feel even more personal and inviting.

DINING ROOMS

Dining rooms for me are all about crowding friends around the table for some delish food, decent wine and a crackling fire in the grate, or simply enjoying a cosy supper with Graham at the end of a long day.

Creating the right atmosphere is key. Too often I see the ubiquitous big table, matching chairs, some sort of pendant in the middle and that is pretty much it! Years ago, I went to a friend's house who had exactly that (except swap out the pendant for a whole load of recessed downlights). Supper was served. I got through the appetiser and then I had to say something (which I realise was extremely bad form on my part, but I felt I was about to undergo surgery, the lighting was so bright!). So I said something. Or rather I did something: dimmed the lights, found some candles, smattered them around the place, and then we continued eating. At least I did, everyone else was a little aghast. Hey, don't ask me over for supper. In fact, thinking about it, no one ever does anymore!

I don't care how the furnishings look (well I do), but atmosphere is super easy to create, by just dimming a few lights and lighting some candles. Little effort, big impact!

It takes skill to put together an eclectic blend of furniture, colour, pattern and texture, and Sue Miller demonstrates this in abundance. No formulaic following of rules here. Her visual risk-taking has created an exciting, warm dining space.

Brown partners perfectly with almost any other colour. In hospitality maven Brent Bolthouse's pad, it communicates a slow down, relax and get comfy vibe, and packs a big visual wallop, simply by making every other hue stand out and look far cooler than it actually is.

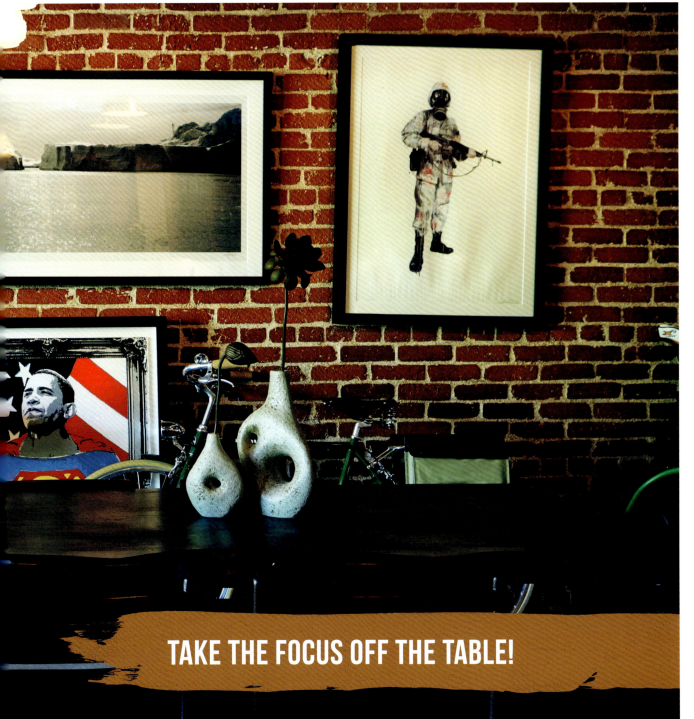

TAKE THE FOCUS OFF THE TABLE!

To create a conversation-worthy dining room, there are many tricks of the trade. And, as ever, colour plays an integral part.

Start by mixing up the chairs. Firstly it will funk up the space and secondly it will allow you to create a more casual ambience. I mismatch in pairs: it gives me that eclectic vibe I'm after, and yet it feels somehow more glamorous.

Rather than having every chair a different hue, rein in the palette by keeping the colours similar and mixing up the textures. So place a wicker chair next to a metal one, an upholstered model next to a wooden seat – that kind of thing.

Sue Miller's individual take on a
kitchen bar feels industrial, raw,
quirky and fabulous.

trust me

A large wooden table serves as the main focal point in Alina Prediado's dining area, with wooden elements in the kitchen tying everything together.

IN MY BOOK, YOU CAN MIX ANYTHING WITH ANYTHING — FURNITURE STYLES, FABRICS, ARTWORK. THE TRICK IS TO UNIFY THE WHOLE LOOK WITH COLOUR. SIMPLE, NO?

Repeating colours throughout will give your dining room extra kudos and make the scheme far more cohesive. In my home, I've got blue leather dining chairs looking through to two lounge armchairs in a slightly more vibrant blue, a big blue oil painting and, whenever I can source them, blue hydrangeas. They echo each other beautifully.

You can also echo the colours with rugs, vases, lamps. Once you get the idea, it's pretty easy to pull off this look. Because the table is the main focal point, the trick here is to take the attention away from it (no matter how cool your table might be!). It takes a little bit of skill, but it will make even an everyday supper seem infinitely more special if there are other things going on in the space.

I always add a centrepiece, which for me is always and forever flowers. There is something about an empty dining table I just don't like, but pop a bunch of bright blooms – however small or tall – in the centre and suddenly you've taken the room to new heights.

This well-dressed, simply accessorised dining area mixes glamour with grandeur, thanks to the huge windows elevating the drama in Athena Calderone's pad.

BEDROOMS

Bedrooms are not the easiest rooms to get right. In fact, I'd go so far as to say they suffer from bland room syndrome. We spend a lot of time, money and thought on living rooms, kitchens, even bathrooms, yet the bedroom is often left bare, painted out in a beige haze of nothingness, with not a lot else going on.

I've struggled with mine (and that is putting it politely). Until recently, it felt sterile and somewhere I would never linger in longer than was necessary. Now it's my sanctuary. I run here when the day gets too crazy, just for a moment's peace, to recalibrate the mind. I hang out here at the weekend, flicking through the papers. I love it! And what made the difference? You guessed it, COLOUR!

I don't know about you guys, but I want my bedroom to soothe and relax me. But that doesn't mean I've opted for the ubiquitous white palette. You can find the most calming combos with dark inky hues, even colour-studded palettes can soothe.

Subtle shades are tempered by sensuous materials and textures, creating a peaceful space that feels beautiful and refined.

A 1970s dressing table ramps up the girliness in this bedroom. Its clean lines (not stereotypically feminine) guarantees it fits in with the rest of the scheme.

Left: A large flirty chandelier and ornate bed lighten the industrial brick wall in Sue Miller's bedroom. The unexpected mix of styles is beyond beautiful.

DREAM SCHEMES

A good place to start your colour scheme is the bed, namely because it takes up the largest amount of space. As a fan of the dark side, I've gone for dark linen, embellished with throws. Another option (seen opposite) is to elevate standard white linen by piling on pillows and mixing patterns: small motifs with large, florals with geometrics, that sort of thing. Make your own headboard from MDF (a cinch!) and cover it in a luxe velvet.

Next, add rugs. However cool your bed, providing another focal point in the room means there's another element for the eye to alight on, and be intrigued by. Rugs anchor rooms, set the tone and add instant glamour; plus, toes touching a beautiful, fluffy rug in the morning is a good thing. Once again, pattern will add instant pizzazz here. Rugs or carpets in solid hues can drain a room's energy. If you do have plain carpets, just skim the odd rug over them – the Americans do it all the time and it looks amazing.

Use lighting to up the ante. Somehow we have to balance practical task lights (for reading, grooming and so on), with spots of mood-altering atmospheric lighting (see pages 106–7). When selecting decorative lighting, don't be too practical with the finish. Choose a tantalising base (mine are either bronze or flocked); you need some small luxurious details that add instant magic to any bedroom.

Bedside tables are another game changer. If possible, vary the heights of these and the colour. I tend to avoid bedside tables and instead use occasional tables, as they are higher than standard ones, lending my space that unexpected twist of grandeur. It doesn't take much to up the style ratings and create one of the cosiest, most relaxing rooms in the whole space.

Tempered with unexpected elements, like the flag and mismatched cushions, the pressed tin ceiling adds to this bedroom's theatricality.

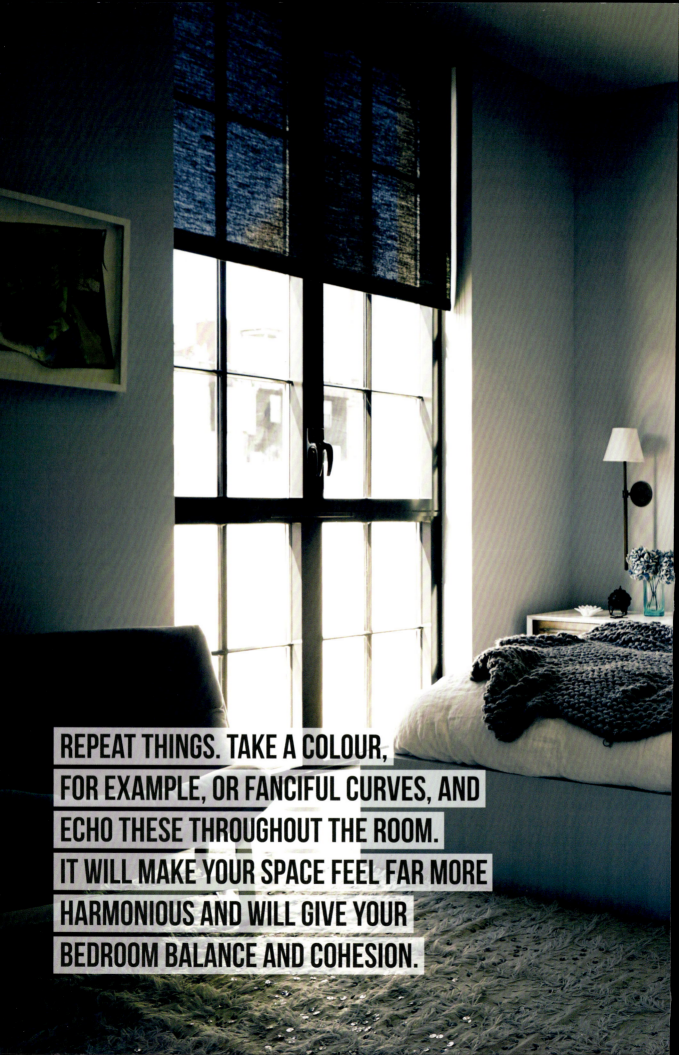

REPEAT THINGS. TAKE A COLOUR,
FOR EXAMPLE, OR FANCIFUL CURVES, AND
ECHO THESE THROUGHOUT THE ROOM.
IT WILL MAKE YOUR SPACE FEEL FAR MORE
HARMONIOUS AND WILL GIVE YOUR
BEDROOM BALANCE AND COHESION.

Athena Calderone's bedroom uses a subtle palette, picked out in the cushions and throws. It feels dreamy but also impactful, thanks to the painting dominating the bedroom wall.

STUDIES

Colour, as we all know, effects how you think, feel and behave, so whether you have a dedicated study room or your spare bedroom double duties as a creative den, getting the colours right actually impacts on the success of your business or your work. Scary stuff, no?

In my experience, the home office is invariably the most neglected space in our homes when it comes to colour. Why? Because most of us still presume that a work space needs to feel 'officey' rather than somewhere we actively want to hang out; somewhere relaxing, stylish, fun, as well as – my most hated word on the planet! – functional.

TO FIND OUT IF YOUR STUDY IS WORKING, ASK YOURSELF HOW IT MAKES YOU FEEL. IF YOUR SPACE ISN'T COLOUR-BALANCED, I SUSPECT THE ANSWER IS, A LITTLE OFF-KILTER.

A luxurious, tactile enclosure with piles of books, a quirky rug and beautiful lighting. The unified palette on the walls and floor allows the accessories to have major impact.

Speaking from experience, the minute I painted my work space out in dark black was the minute I improved my mood, increased my productivity and felt way more creative.

Figuring out your palette should be easy, once you consider the emotional impact that colour brings. We each have our own personal connections to colour. When I think of deep brown, for example, I think of squishy comforting rooms that make me feel protected from the outside world.

Red, on the other hand, is a fab colour for increasing the heart rate and capturing one's attention (perfect for a home office, no?). Injecting some sheen makes me feel super powerful. Plus it lifts the energy! Or you might be running a hectic biz and need a space that feels calm and focused, in which case you should opt for something more subtle. Yellow, one of the most overlooked colours in the spectrum, is ideal for adding warmth.

Pay attention to the intensity of the colour, as this is key in establishing mood: strong brights stimulate, low saturated colours soothe. Beware of the rainbow effect: such a profusion of colours that you walk into a room and feel confused. But remember, there are no wrong colours: success is all down to how you use your palette and what makes you feel the most productive.

TIME TO GET TO WORK!

If using a one-colour background scheme, up the ante with some contrasting pops. A gold office chair adds instant drama. Amazing!

A large black table stands in stark contrast to the white walls, but noir accents (via the accessories and frames) add a further chic visual effect.

Left: Even though the shelves are packed full with books and pictures, the room feels calm thanks to the dark palette. Inky hues give you license to go a little wild. Check out the fancy sculpture on the desk.

OUTDOOR ROOMS

You should never be able to read a space instantly; instead you should design it so that the eye is pulled in many different directions.

Believe it or not, one of the best ways to make your inside space look and feel bigger is to decorate your outside space, thereby extending the vista. I'm not talking about adding a few additional pots here, I mean you should decorate your space like an outdoor room, even if it's the tiniest of areas.

We have a double height glass extension in our pad that opens fully onto our walled London garden, so getting the outdoor space right has been really important. Sitting inside, you feel like you can actually touch the garden. It feels very jumbly, almost jungle-like. I've made sure that everything is overgrown. Once outside, you have to delve in to see what's there, but that's the golden rule!

The thing is, decorating outdoors is exactly the same thing as decorating indoors: you need layers. If you clock your garden or balcony or roof terrace in an instant, it will read as boring. Whereas if you have quite a bit going on, it tantalises the eye because you don't know where to look.

Biggest trick for turning outdoor
spaces around? Rethink your lighting.
These beautifully strung lights elevate
the space year-round in Athena
Calderone's rooftop garden.

Make the outdoors as informal as you can by adding layers, like this sweet little table in the backyard of Brent Bolthouse's pad.

TAKE YOUR CUE FROM INSIDE

People get a bit scared about using colour in the garden, but when you add a pop on a wall, go off-radar with your fence colour, or plump for a piece of furniture in a zingy hue, it takes outdoor spaces to a whole other dimension. Accessorise them like you would your living room with lights, candles, the odd pouf, cushions, lanterns, so it feels like this cool hang-out zone.

I've picked up old tables from flea markets; apple crates, which I upturn and use as outdoor coffee tables, along with a collection of eclectic chairs – some of them modern, some of them country rustic. Lumps of old wood double duty as occasional tables. I've strung tealights in trees, and lanterns abound.

RETHINK YOUR COLOURS

- When it comes to decorating outside, I would recommend you go darker than you would indoors, because full-on daylight can make certain hues less impressive. When not covered in foliage, the walls in my garden are black, complementing the green beautifully.

- I tend to use very few bright hues in the garden: furniture is either black or grey, apart from a couple of bright yellow, slatted metal chairs under the fig tree at the back. In warmer climes, bright colours look refreshing; in our softer light, they can look a bit tawdry if you're not careful.

- Olives, browns, burnt umbers and greens look amazing.

- In my pad all flowerpots are bronze – they bounce the light around beautifully.

THINK BIG

If you can, go the whole hog and create an actual outdoor room – think outdoor kitchen, fireplace, loungy chairs: the works. It makes the space feel supremely luxurious. Friends think I'm bonkers, because even in the depths of winter there we are, all wrapped up, sitting by the outdoor fireplace on a weekend winter's afternoon, a fire in the grate, a stew slowly cooking in the Dutch oven. I love it!

Whether you've got a porch, a big backyard or a tiny space, decorate with bright abandon. Do that and I guarantee you'll be outdoors in all weathers. See you out there!

Decorate your outside world like
your inside space, as you can see
here. Sofa, sweet little coffee table
and a couple of chairs – perfect!

BE AUD

ACIOUS

STATEMENT PIECES

Let's set the record straight, shall we? I don't just run into a space, sprinkle a bit of fairy dust over it and suddenly magic happens. I use insider tricks, so that if you happen to enter one of my rooms it feels sophisticated, inspirational and creative. The best trick in my book? Well, that's easy. Statement pieces, of course!

The whole point of a statement piece is pretty self-explanatory. It makes a statement in that it immediately pulls your eye towards it. It can help define a space; add a splash of colour or pattern; maybe highlight something decorative. It's a super-easy way to express your aesthetic.

The idea here is to ditch convention, go a little off radar and indulge in what you love. I have a big heavy console in front of the window that we have to heave out and in every morning and evening to open and close the shutters. I have another console in the hallway that makes a certain part of it so narrow you kind of have to breath in to pass by. Still, I like how they look.

More is more. Ditch having one focal point in a room and have at least two if not three. It tantalises the eye that way. Take this space (opposite): if there was only one statement piece, the room wouldn't feel complex enough. Add a few and you've nailed it.

Listen to your gut. If your gut says it's feeling too much, do what I do and clear everything out. Start with a blank canvas and re-introduce. Otherwise, sit back and enjoy the results!

Left: Add a dose of drama through your accessories to give your space a bit of ooh-la-la.

Below: Who knew that a kitchen door could look so cool? A faux marble paint effect on the door, partnered with a gilded painting, feels to me like this apartment's raison d'être!

Below left: Nothing says conversational piece more than a sculpture, and when it's crafted out of granite it becomes a focal point in its own right.

Right: Think of a room in layers. Visual interest comes through layering different materials and textures together. It also comes through staggering the heights of your display objects.

HAVE A FEW STATEMENT PIECES AND BUILD EVERYTHING ELSE AROUND THEM.

P+P (PERSPECTIVE AND PROPORTION)

To create those magical *Alice in Wonderland* interiors that I do all the time, mixing up the P&P is one of the most vital components in the decorating puzzle.

What I'm trying to do, whenever I start designing a space, is to disorientate you, to give you the impression that you've fallen down the rabbit hole into this curious world, where everything looks a bit strange, and the eye doesn't know what to focus on. So I play around with scale; plonk tall vases next to smaller ones; arrange blocky, square-looking ceramics next to curvaceous sculptures.

Statement pieces won't truly shine unless you create tension, remember! And tension creates intrigue. So mix hard with soft, feminine with masculine. I've got a flocked parrot lamp in an intoxicating shot of lime on my console next to a big old concrete vase. The oversized vase is a statement in its own right; the parrot is smaller, but the colour grabs the eye. Fab-u-lous!

The great thing about introducing statement pieces is that they distract the eye from any problems the room may have, like it's a funny shape or has ugly cupboards or horrible radiators – statement pieces take away from the mundane.

The biggest trick to remember is that if you only have one statement piece your room won't feel complex enough, but more than three or four can feel messy. So have a few statements and then build the rest of the room around them. It's a bit like pulling together an outfit really.

You have to have confidence when you add statement pieces, like this beautiful supersized mirror. The way to pull it off is to make sure it blends with the rest of your furnishings. Here, the mirror has a strong classic style, so it's the size that's played up rather than the colour.

Deep saturated shades
complement the unusual mix
of furniture, including this
beautiful woven African chair
draped with a leopard hide.
The composition is elevated
further by a cool painting
and a giant cactus.

DO

- Think small (as well as big). A statement piece doesn't have to be huge to make a statement.

- Make a statement with colour, pattern and texture – size isn't everything.

- Mix up materials and styles, because we want to create tension, remember!

- Make sure the ugly paraphernalia of everyday life – the remotes, coins and keys – goes away; only the cool stuff stays out.

- Look at your styled arrangement from above. Stand on a chair; it will give you a totally different bird's eye perspective, and if it works from up high I promise you it will work from the ground. **EASY PEASY LITTLE TRICK!**

DON'T

- Don't be practical! The minute you go down that route is the minute your space becomes boring. Follow your heart and not your head.

- Don't fall into the trap of thinking your statement pieces have to be the same size or scale. So, for example, be wary of hanging a massive painting over a great big sofa. **BIG YAWN!**

- Don't worry about the shape of your room or the ugliness of your fittings – statement pieces take away from the mundane!

- Don't go overboard with too many statement pieces – it can feel like a hot mess.

Add an element of quirk – like this glass/ceramic monkey – to your vignette and it immediately lightens the mood.

Left: You can mix anything with anything if you rein in the colour palette. Controlled chaos I call it, but it works every time. A black-and-white scheme brings magic to this coffee table, rug and vessels.

MASTERING THE MIXED LOOK

Hunker down into any style magazine across the globe and you'll see the eclectic, mix-and-match look is in. To me, it's the best style as it's just so genuine and unsnobbish. It's an extremely hard thing to pull off, as nothing matches and yet your space has to make perfect sense and feel beautiful, calming, glam, and sophisticated, rather than bonkers. But don't let that worry you: here's how to do it with panache!

FIND A COMMON DENOMINATOR.
Find a thread to hold your scheme seamlessly together – it could be a paint colour, textural feature or your choice of furnishings. Isolated pops against a more neutral or sludgy palette look amazing. Or you could link disparate elements through material – concrete, wood, slubby soft wool. A unifying element will leave you the freedom to fill your home with the things you love.

LIMIT YOUR STATEMENTS.
If you're referencing multiple time periods and styles, not everything in the room should be statement-worthy, otherwise your space will look and feel a little bonkers. Limit yourself to a few statement pieces, then add some laid-back accessories that quietly do their job – think chunky vases, little glass tealights, the odd piece of sculpture in an inky or neutral palette. Beautiful additions, but with no ego attached.

This beautiful original console
brings intrigue at every glance.

When it comes to choosing accessories, don't think too much. Just grab what you love. These eagles add an instant friendly form to this space.

Right: It's the pared-down palette that makes the eclectic style feel beautiful, not chaotic. The floor-to-ceiling bookcase in my pad nails it because there are very few colour pops.

THINK IN TWOS.
To rock a mashed-up style, you need to create a sense of balance. For example, you can't expect a Chinese dresser, a rococo mirror, an Italian table, a retro chair, a Victorian painting and a modern rug to gel if they are all different materials and hues. A nice trick I use is to add things in pairs: two retro chairs and a few modern rugs will harmonise the whole look, making a space feel calmer and more cohesive. So by all means have a hodgepodge of styles; just remember to double a few styles up.

ADD SOME GLUE.
Pieces that glue a room together magically are rugs and cushions – so pay particular attention to these. You'll be amazed at how effective they can be in tying everything in!

EXPECT A LOT OF TRIAL & ERROR.
This is true when decorating in any style, but especially true with the eclectic look. The process takes time. I'm forever pulling things in and then pulling them out a second later. But don't be intimidated. Yes, it takes time to get right, but doesn't anything worthwhile?

IT'S ALL
ABOUT VISUAL
JUXTAPOSITION
AND AN
ABUNDANCE
OF FUN!

This pad is rule-breaking with its fearless graphic use of colour. The cleverness is in the impact of that one blue wall, adding immediate depth and intrigue without feeling over the top. Throw in some modern art and a few irreverent touches, and you have something totally unique, skillful and unexpected.

FAB FLOORS

Good design starts from the ground up, so selecting the right floor is one of the biggest design decisions you will ever make. Your floor is the largest surface in a room, which means it has the potential to dictate your overall aesthetic. Plus, it has to feel beautiful, look amazing and be functional all at the same time.

A BIG ASK?

When I first moved into my house, we were faced with dingy scratched floors, a bit of beaten-up lino and horrible carpet, so I know only too well how daunting it feels to crack the code for flooring. However, get it right and not only will your floor add value to your home, it will also pull your entire room together.

The good news is that virtually all types of modern flooring – from lino to tile, from wood to carpet to polished concrete – will last for years, so this decision really can be more personality-driven than anything else.

LOCATION IS KEY

Location is super-important when it comes to your choice of flooring. By which I mean, where is the flooring going? Is the area wet or semi-wet (like a bathroom or loo)? Does it get a lot of foot traffic (like a hallway)? Does it need to absorb sound, and/or keep warm and cool air from escaping? Finally, are you looking for easy-to-maintain, no-fuss practicality; comfort and a touch of luxury; or a bit of both? Considering these factors will help narrow down your selection.

HARD 'V' SOFT

Hard floors are easy to clean, but cold underfoot. (In which case, it's worth figuring out if you can add underfloor heating – amazing in the winter, I have to say!) Carpets are soft underfoot but take longer to vacuum and are less easy to clean.

Patterned tiles lend instant pizzazz to this tiny Parisian kitchen, turning the eye away from how small the space is to how cool the vibe is. Genius!

TREADING THE BOARDS

If, like me, you are lucky enough to find some classic floorboards under layers of carpet or lino, these can be sanded down to look as good as new. Varnished or painted, the light that reflects off floorboards will lend a beautiful glow to your space. Plus, any knocks or scuffs simply add to the character.

If you're in the market for new boards, source the widest planks possible as it makes floors look way more expensive. Another tip is to paint out the boards exactly the same shade as your walls, so that whatever you put on them will instantly pop. I've done it and it's a game changer!

LOVELY LAMINATE

Laminate has suffered a bad rap in the past (too many orange-tinged panels out there), but don't rule it out. Whether you go for a wood-, stone- or ceramic-looking laminate, the best quality stuff is good value, fab in high traffic areas and resistant to scuffing and scratching, which makes it very low maintenance. Look out for laminate flooring that comes in interlocking planks and needs no glue, as it's easy enough to install this yourself.

If you're in the market for a wood-look laminate, remember that it should look and feel exactly like the real thing. Manufacturers now offer exotic woods and unique finishes, rustic textures and unusual grains, plus a great selection of colours, ranging from the palest almost-white to deep walnut-brown.

The thicker the laminate, the better, especially when it comes to unlevel spots in your subfloor (thicknesses go all the way from 7mm to 12mm). Check out the AC (abrasion class) rating, which is applied to every line of laminate floor, to indicate the product's durability. The higher the number, the harder wearing the floor. For example, AC1 flooring is designed for residential areas with light traffic, like the bedroom. AC5 laminate is designed for commercial applications. Finally, look at the warranty, which can be anything from 10 years to a lifetime.

Rugs are the base of the room and I'm crushing this combo: an animal hide hanging out with a woolen number. One makes a statement, the other quietly gets on with its job!

RUGS OVER RUGS

The biggest game-changing trick I can give you is to opt for a rug or carpet with a small motif or pattern. Pattern – no matter how small – adds instant pizzazz!

I am obsessed with rugs (not so much carpets), as their transformative powers are second to none. I use them to cosy up and create zones in my open plan space. I love rugs with texture and natural fibres – slubby, shaggy, flat weave, sisal, leather, cotton, wool, jute – it's a pretty endless list. Don't worry about finding one to fit from wall to wall. Buy a few and layer rugs over rugs (and patterns over solids) to ramp up the cosiness and create a unique dialogue in your space.

Opt for wool wherever possible as it outlasts all the synthetic counterparts. I have gotten many of my rugs from flea markets and auction houses. I've picked up a huge Sixties Moroccan rug for £140, numerous rugs for the hallway for a little over £50, and – bargain-of-all-bargains – a massive one for the bedroom at £120 (for my favourite stockists, see page 234). If you happen to have more than one rug going on in a room as I do, restrict the colour palette and then you can mix far more easily.

The Moroccan rug makes this den cosy and complete, creating a subtle texture with its natural yarns.

TERRIFIC TILES

Durable, practical and beautiful all at the same time, a ceramic or porcelain tile floor might push your budget a little, but on the plus side it will last a lifetime, even in wet areas (like bathrooms and kitchens), or heavy-traffic areas (like your entry hall). If I had my time again, I would tile our hallway. The amount of dirt and mess the two Ms bring in from their walks would be swept up in a jiffy with a patterned, under-heated floor.

With a plethora of colours, sizes, styles and finishes to choose from, a tiled floor is a clever way to personalise your look, and add colour and intrigue to any room. Opt for a bold pattern and keep the rest of the scheme low key. Or try porcelain tiles if you like the look of natural stone but want to save money, or are looking for something a bit more hardwearing and durable than the real thing.

As we know, the big trend in interiors right now is eclecticism, meaning anything goes, so whether you want a uniform flooring scheme throughout or a medley of styles, it's entirely up to you. Liberating stuff, hey!

If your room is small, a repeated colour
(or different shades of the same colour)
will have a cohesive effect – check out
the green chair and green wall here.

THREE WAYS
TO COLOUR YOUR FLOORS

Light floors 'v' dark floors: which one to choose? It's a personal preference (as decorating always is), just don't forget to answer the question. The right colour under foot is one of the easiest ways to create magic, drama and intrigue in your home!

1. Dark floors offer drama, opulence, sophistication and glamour. They may show up the dirt and pet hairs horribly, but on the plus side they make rooms appear cosier. And I happen to believe they work anywhere, from the bedroom to the loo.

2. Light floors, on the other hand, are an excellent choice if you have pale walls as they will harmonise and blend into your scheme, opening up your space and giving it a calm, laidback vibe. Also, they are much better at hiding dirt and dust.

3. My favourite option is to **paint floors, walls, ceilings, trims and doors in the same hue.** I want my floor to recede, so that when I plop a rug or furniture on it, everything pings.

When I select rugs for my pad (pictured here) I gravitate towards patterns where less is more. The subtler the motif, the more I can mix up my furniture styles!

TRANSFORMATIVE STYLING TIPS

I think it's odd how some designers are a bit funny about giving away their tricks. I guess it's the same way that people are when you ask them where they got something and you get that 'oh I don't remember' line! I suppose it's all about distinguishing yourself from the crowd and protecting ideas and sources. On the contrary, if an idea or source has worked for me, I am only too happy and excited to share it with you guys, so it gives you just as much pleasure as me.

I digress: this section is all about transformative decorating tips and below are my most dramatic ones.

SUPERSIZE YOUR ARTWORK OR FURNITURE

Anything supersized will add grandeur. With artwork, for me it's seldom about the medium (for example, oil 'v' print), it's about the size. The minute you large-scale anything is the minute you add more intrigue and kudos to your home. It works beautifully with furniture, too. I've just swapped out a little green tub chair in my studio for a big, winged leather chair that is way too big for the space, flanking my bookshelf wall. And suddenly a magical vibe has been cast next to my desk. Things don't have to be in proportion. The more you ditch the rules, the more interesting your space becomes.

SMALL CHANGES CAN HAVE THE BIGGEST IMPACT!

Little things like swapping ugly plastic light switches for metal ones, or replacing nasty door handles with ceramic ones, give rooms an instant upgrade. Painting out radiators and skirting boards the same colour as your walls is another small change that has the greatest impact!

ADD A NOOK

Incorporating a seating nook into a bedroom or a living room, away from the main conversational area, looks and feels so sweet, plus it makes your space feel instantly more intriguing.

EMBRACE THE SEASONS

I don't want to live in a year-round summer. Does that sound crazy? I like seasons. I want to put on a hefty coat and go trample and chase leaves in Hyde Park with the two Ms in autumn; I want to light fires in winter; I want to pair back the sheepskins and slubby cushions in the spring, and maybe take them away altogether for summer, adding in some brighter pops.

Embrace the seasons by swapping up the foliage and flowers in your pad, and by changing your scents from floral and light to woody and smoky. It will make you feel happy to be at home at any time of the year and ensure that your space evolves (very subtly) rather than staying the same.

GO FOR GOLD

I know the whole gold trend has been done a lot, but I can't get enough of it,. No matter if your vibe is trad or contemporary, adding a little bling makes spaces feel super swanky. Think pineapple sconces on the walls, think gold mirrors or frames, gold adds such a classy note!

HANG LOW

Hang pendant lights or chandeliers lower than you normally would over tables. I've literally just done this and it looks amazing. Rather than the chandelier floating near the top of the ceiling, it's actually become a major accessory in its own right, and helps anchor the room. All because I lowered it a tad!

USE BOOKS AS PART OF YOUR TABLESCAPE

Adding little heaps of books to occasional tables and consoles is something I do all the time. It's a small thing but it adds a huge impact. Plop a candle on top or a posy of flowers and watch it add intrigue, pattern and life. Nailed!

Michelle James's Brooklyn living room has an air of expansiveness thanks to its calm neutral colours. The varying shades mean it's a palette you can constantly come back to and never tire of.

DETAILS
(THE FANTASTIC FIVE)

Details take homes to the next level: they are such game changers. I'm talking flowers, candles, plants, objects, cushions, books – all those little things that I can never get enough of.

As with your statement pieces, finishing touches are never about practicality. You can't think, why put a vase on a mantle if there are no flowers in it. Or why put three cushions on a sofa when I don't need any? Or, looking at my mantle right now as I type, why put a stone head and a gold head next to each other?

I've got more chairs than a school room and more flowers than a florist, I reckon. Makes no sense, but makes my heart race. Here are my five favourite tips for bringing rooms to life.

1 ADD A BIT OF UGLY

I know this sounds odd, but stay with me for a second. If everything looks 'too done' a space can feel uptight. So if you've got the odd accessory that is less than beautiful, say a painting with a chipped frame or a vase with a dull colour, this can actually ground a room. I think a lot of people don't realise that a room with everything (from colours to furniture) perfectly coordinated looks saccharine. There is value in having something a bit thread bare, a bit of patina from a vessel, or a rustic table with peeling paint next to a cool polished-looking sofa. It actually tones the overall look down and will make your space feel more lived-in and relaxed. Add a dark edge: not everything should be pretty!

2 GET COSY

All those pieces that make a home feel comfy, like soft pillows, throws, old rugs and baskets, actually humanise your space and add layers of warmth to a room. The less you embrace them, the more one-dimensional your space will look, so in my book you can never have enough. Ditch having things in rows and instead cross things over, butt them up against each other and leave no gaps.

3 EMBRACE BLACK

I am not simply saying this as a lover of the dark side. When you add a touch of black to your accessories – think vases, rugs, lamps – you'll be adding instant sophisticated glamour and intrigue. Promise!

INJECT A TOUCH OF JOLLY

Every room needs something jolly in it to lift your spirits. Those little personal smalls that no designer could ever buy in – kids' drawings, animal figurines, little finishing touches that you've accumulated along the way – bring us meaning and joy. Put a flocked bison head on the walls, or a poodle lamp on an ostrich table, like I have in my studio. The most memorable and the best interiors all have elements of fun in them. They tell a narrative and that narrative doesn't always have to make sense, it just has to loosen up the vibe. There's nothing worse in my book than walking into an uptight room!

4

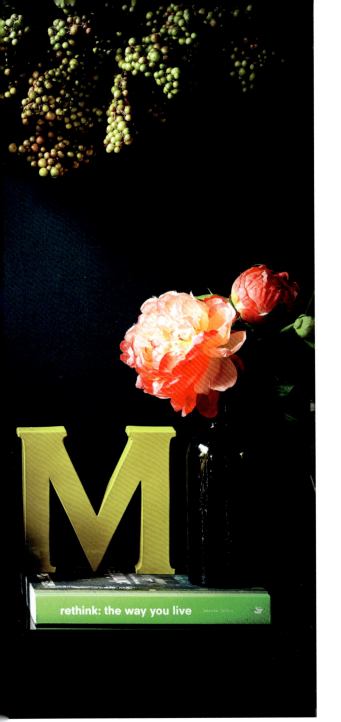

5

HAVE THE RIGHT ATTITUDE

This is my ultimate tip. Great style doesn't come from owning a particular object or accessory, it comes from having a great attitude: a relaxed laissez faire-ness, if that makes sense. Whatever your style, it's all about creating a home that feels inviting and tantalising, charming and relaxed for you and your family. You can't do that simply by choosing the right accessory. The details are extremely important to a space – I know the difference they've made to mine, elevating my mood, making me want to throw my doors open and entertain every night; making me more creative even. But it's not the objects themselves that have done this, it's more the way I've approached the decorating, with a relaxed attitude of not taking it all too seriously. So I've created this layered and rich, quirky and amazing home that feels comfortable and magical and totally unique to me.

YOU DON'T NEED TO HIRE A DESIGNER TO CREATE AN AMAZING HOME. YOU JUST NEED TO START THINKING LIKE ONE. AND WHEN YOU BREAK IT DOWN, THAT'S PRETTY EASY, RIGHT?

THE UNDERTONES

A fresh coat of paint will always be the easiest, most transformative thing you can do to your space. You can turn gloomy rooms into stately abodes, cabins into palaces – there is no other more cost-effective way of turning something around. Luckily for us, we're in the middle of a paint revolution, with a ton of dazzling new hues, textures and finishes to help reinvigorate or reinvent our homes.

As tempting as it sounds to cheap out on paint, this really is a big no no. Expensive paints are made from natural pigments from the earth – clay, sand, stone, soft rocks – which the colour spectrometer (for all its perfect tints) can never match. They have incredible depth, redolence, and layers and layers of colour underlying the paint's mass colour.

These beautiful undertones, which subtly change with the light, can cause a great deal of confusion when it comes to choosing paint (trust me, I know!), as the complexity of the pigment makes each paint

absolutely unique. When choosing a colour then, the trick is to figure out if you veer towards the warm or the cool end of the spectrum. Let's take blue as an example. Say you favour warm tones, you need to look for a blue that contains some reddish undertones, which to your eye will appear more plum. Opt for a cool blue and you'll notice nuances of green and teal.

Since most colours are actually combinations of other colours – for example, red and yellow combine to make orange – the majority of paints are made up of many complex pigments, oodles of depth and undertones. All of which effect the final hue.

Read on for my ultimate tips on paint, which are going to save you time, frustration and spondoolies. First up, testing!

TEST, TEST AND TEST AGAIN

When it comes to judging paint, never ever, ever just go by the swatch card. It won't do the colour justice or remotely reflect how it will look in your pad. For that, you're going to need to paint out the hugest area you can with a sample pot. Don't opt out and paint a bit of board or the back of some roll of wallpaper and think that's enough. It isn't! You need to test the colour on a whole wall. It's the best insurance I can give you.

Above: The fire engine red walls in this games room don't seem over the top because the hue has been incorporated into the artwork, cushions and billiard table, making the transition less about contrast and more about ease.

Right: A custom wallpaper, crafted with gold and pearly grey horizontal lines, transforms the dining room of Jean-Louis Deniot's Parisian apartment. It's one of the most tantalising combos I have seen.

- When you open the tin, don't judge the colour, as it will dry so much darker. Sample it on the wall first, let it dry and then decide.

- Paint different areas in your test hue. That way you will see how the colour looks with sunlight, daylight, fluorescent light, halogen light – all of which affect the hue differently!

- Don't just dab on one coat, as this will never give you the intensity and depth you need. This is doubly true if you are going dark.

- Don't scrimp on paint brands (it's worth repeating this point!). The more expensive you go with your paint, the more expensive your walls will look. The minute you slap that cheap, synthetic paint on your walls is the minute it disappoints.

I would rather spend my money on a cool chandelier or a chair or an amazing rug than on a decorator. It's a personal choice – which many times I've questioned, late at night over a beer, so darn tired it nearly did me in. Here are the tricks I've learnt along the way – the hard way you might say! Hopefully, if you're thinking of changing up your colour palette, these might make it a little bit easier.

GIVE YOUR PAINT A GOOD STIR

Everybody knows this, right? You have to stir your pot of paint before you begin. The more you stir, the smoother it will be when applied.

BUY AN EXTENSION POLE

A telescoping extension pole for your paint roller saves endless trips up and down the ladder. Essential for painting ceilings!

DON'T CLEAN THE BRUSH

I don't mean like ever, I mean if you happen to be painting again tomorrow. Wrap your brush and trays in cling film or foil. Works a treat.

GET CRAFTY WITH FOIL

If you're painting a door and don't want to go to the hassle of removing handles, wrap the doorknob in aluminium foil. That way you can paint right up to the knob with no gaps.

7 STEPS TO THE PERFECT PAINT JOB

Don't freak out when I tell you there are seven steps to preparing a wall for painting. I know that sounds like a huge bore, but preparing surfaces for paint will save you a lot of hassle in the long run.

STEP ONE: Sounds obvious I know, but get as much stuff out of the room as you possibly can. When you are painting you don't want to be manoeuvring around a ton of stuff.

STEP TWO: Wipe over the walls with a feather duster to clean away any cobwebs, dust, etc.

STEP THREE: Fill in any nail holes, or cracks, with lightweight filler. Allow to dry, then sand. Apply a second coat of filler, if needed, and sand again.

STEP FOUR: Clean the walls with sugar soap and a sponge.

STEP FIVE: Tape off adjacent walls, woodwork and light switches with painter tape to protect surfaces.

STEP SIX: Prime or undercoat. Apply a primer if you are painting a new surface, like freshly plastered walls. If you are painting an existing painted wall, use an undercoat. They both play an important part in your topcoat looking top notch.

TURN GLOOMY STATELY

FINISHES

It's a minefield out there with so many paint finishes to choose from. Let me be your official guide!

A while back, we had two choices: water- or oil-based paint. Water-based paints have less VOCs (volatile organic compounds) so they are quick-drying, easy to clean and they don't yellow. The purists out there (I'm kind of one of them) will tell you that, although they are fab, they don't have quite the same depth as gloss, nor are they as durable or hardwearing. That said, the majority of wall paint is water-based. Oil-based paint is still popular for woodwork, like doors, floors and furniture.

One word of warning: if you are working on a surface previously painted with oil-based paints in a water-based finish, you will need to 'key the wall' (painter speak for roughing it up all over) with a smooth-to-medium grit sandpaper. Otherwise your paint will not adhere very well.

In terms of finish, you can opt for a matte or silk emulsion. I am a lover of a super-flat matte – so my walls look and feel like they've been wrapped in velvet – but silk, eggshell and satin finishes have more reflectivity and are often used in demanding environments – think bathrooms and kitchens – where easy clean-up is desired. A light sheen finish is also perfect for a dimly-lit small space, like a powder room or hallway, as it reflects the light.

Finally, gloss has the most reflective sheen. These paints are highly durable, stand up to cleaning and can make the coolest statement. Although, just to warn, make sure your walls are smooth before applying: gloss will highlight any imperfections, big time!

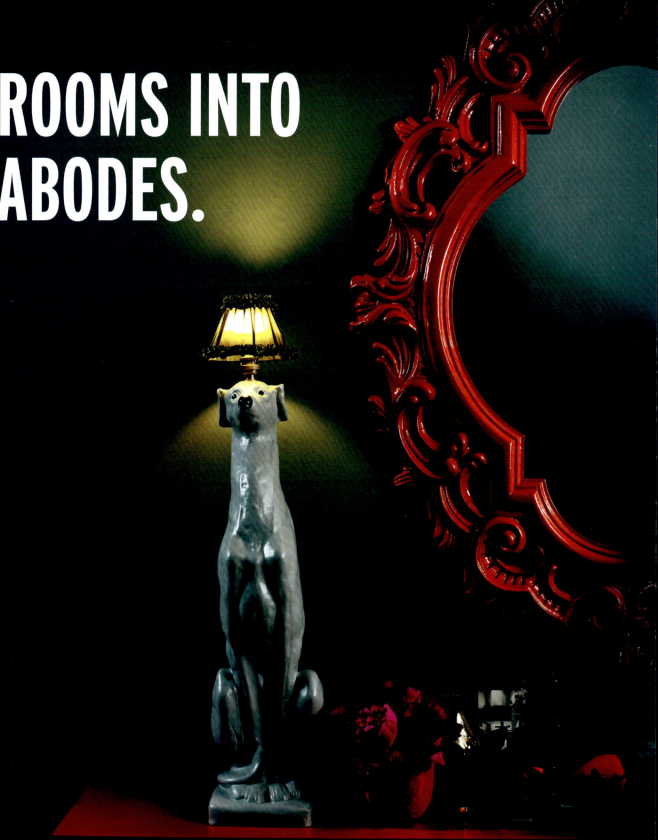

FIGHT THE RULES

If you're painting a small apartment, consider going down the glossy route and add lamps for texture: this adds a sense of volume and makes any space feel instantly impressive.

That old nonsense about smaller rooms needing to be painted in light hues no longer cuts the mustard. Tiny spaces look way more cosy (and den-like) when painted out in sludgy hues. What tiny spaces can't deal with is a jarring array of shades, so keep contrasts to a minimum. While we're at it, ditch the old rule about painting skirts and trim out in a contrasting hue. It just shortens rooms and makes them look stumpy. My trick is to paint everything out in the same hue so your walls look and feel incredibly tall.

Take the plunge and paint your trim dark. Not only does it highlight door and window frames, it adds a dramatic effect without much time or effort. Think of it as eyeliner for the home!

SHOPPING FOR COLOUR

I spend much of my time trawling the globe looking for products or working with factories and artisans who are producing my own label, so I get to do a lot of schlepping all over the world. These are the stores, artists, artisans and bloggers that are continually on my radar.

UK

Anthropologie
www.anthropologie.com
With zillions of stores in the US and now nine in the UK, Anthropologie is a great place to go for homeware: rugs, kitchen stuff, and one-off finds. Plus, check out how they style the stores: lots of colour inspiration to take home.

Atelier Abigail Ahern
www.abigailahern.org
Where I blog, post ideas and add oodles of colour. Whether you're shopping for ceramics, lighting, cushions, furniture or flowers. Atelier Abigail Ahern is possibly the coolest shop on the planet. Can I say that about my own store? Hey ho, I just did!

Aston Mathews
www.astonmatthews.co.uk
Great for cool bathroom finds. If you want to up your style ratings at no extra cost, buy 'bath' taps and install them over your sink. The effect is grander in scale, quirkier and way cooler; it's the thing I get quizzed on most when anyone visits my bathroom!

Caravan
www.caravanstyle.com
My friend, the author and stylist Emily Chalmers owns this fabulous independent shop in Hoxton, with a quirky selection of finds. Shop online or by appointment only.

Debenhams
www.debenhams.com
Affordable cool homeware finds on the high street at great prices, from John Rocha to Ben de Lisi.

Liberty
www.liberty.co.uk
Has a fabulous homeware section on the 4th floor, best for traditional and contemporary pieces with a twist.

Mint
www.mintshop.co.uk
A beautifully created collection of bright, fresh finds, often exclusive to Mint.

Nicole Farhi Home
www.nicolefarhi.com
Beautiful ceramics, coloured glass, furniture, and textiles in the softest of palettes. Expensive but it lasts forever. I brought a big slubby throw from here 16 years ago and it's still laying across my bed.

Ochre
www.ochre.net
A British based furniture, lighting and accessory design company. They have a showroom, open by appointment, in London and a store selling beautiful handmade sofas, armchairs and lighting, in a phenomenally beautiful building in Soho, NYC.

Paul Smith, Albemarle Street
www.paulsmith.co.uk
Paul Smith is a designer I admire beyond belief. Shop here for eclectic British fashion, unique objets d'art and, of course, his signature multi-coloured stripes.

Rockett St George
www.rockettstgeorge.co.uk
Stylish, original and fabulous; I love everything Rockett does.

Sofa.com
www.sofa.com
A vast array of sofas including a selection of pieces I have designed. Yee haw!

Squint

www.squintlimited.com
Best known for her exuberant patchwork designs, my friend Lisa Whatmough, founder and owner of Squint, has the most tantalising array of furniture, accessories, lighting and wallpaper. Everything is richly decorative. I am the hugest fan!

AUSTRALIA

Beacon Lighting

www.beaconlighting.com.au
Don't tell anyone but I'm a bit addicted to Australian renovation shows *The Block* and *House Rules*. The contestants invariably use Beacon Lighting to source everything. The selection looks fab.

Comer & King

www.comerandking.com
My friend Cam Comer is an amazing interior designer and crafter of some seriously cool textiles. The showroom is by appointment only, but don't let that put you off when there are such beautiful cushions, throws and upholstered furniture to purchase. Plus, Cam takes on private commissions all over the world, so if you fancy something unique, he's your man!

David Bromley

www.davidbromley.com.au
www.rebeccahossack.com
I am a big fan of artist David Bromley's work; he combines a pop sensibility with an inventive approach to painting. In Australia his work is readily available and displayed everywhere, from furniture showrooms to restaurants.

For anyone not living in Australia, Rebecca Hossack represents him internationally.

Dinosaur Designs

www.dinosaurdesigns.com
Stocking homeware, furniture, and even jewellery, Dinosaur Designs mixes natural organic with playful, to brilliant effect.

Doug up on Bourke

www.douguponbourke.com.au
Industrial, rustic, laid back – cool for vintage finds, and how can you not visit with a name like that?!

Fenton & Fenton

www.fentonandfenton.com.au
From recycled timber furniture to vivid textiles, from one-off pieces to some amazing artwork, I love Fenton. Not only are the products unique, they all have such a happy vibe. Pieces are sourced from far-flung corners of the globe to much closer to home.

Ici et la

www.icietla.com.au
Full to the brim with European finds, from vibrant striped fabrics to zinc letters to French garden furniture. Like stepping into a cool antiques store in the heart of Paris – except we are in Australia. Amazing! Plus they have a cool dog.

Izzi & Popo

www.izziandpopo.com.au
A great selection of imported vintage finds (mainly from Belgian markets).

Koskela

www.koskela.com.au
Simple but well-crafted furniture and accessories, all made in Australia.

Pony Rider

www.ponyrider.com.au
A solid, stylish range of homewares – cushions, throws, tablecloths and quilts.

The Society Inc, Sibella Court

www.thesocietyinc.com.au
Haberdashery, hardware and super-cool paint colors under the Muroband label. It's teeny tiny and off the beaten track, but well worth a gander.

FRANCE

Astier de Villatte

www.astierdevillatte.com
This beautiful chic Parisian store specialises in tableware: hand-thrown ceramics, organic in feel, and beyond beautiful.

Caravane

www.caravane.fr
Beautiful textiles and homeware worth checking out; there are a couple of stores around Paris.

Merci

www.merci-merci.com
For me this is one of the most fabulous stores in the world. Part used book shop, part café, with a fashion house and interiors emporium in the mix.

GERMANY

Kühn Keramik

www.kuehn-keramik.com
Ceramic art and pottery tableware that is edgy, tongue in cheek and totally ace.

HOLLAND

Mariska Meijers

www.mariskameijers.com
Tantalisingly colourful, the artist Mariska Meijers (whose home is featured in this book) has translated her sassy artwork and prints into uber-cool cushions, wallpapers and trays. Her use of colour is intoxicating.

Moooi

www.moooi.com
The collection of furniture, lighting and accessories is a little tongue-in-cheek, if not bonkers (life-size horses crafted from resin as a floor light, anyone?) Still, every home must have a dash of oddness to take it to another level and these guys will set you on your way!

ITALY

Rossana Orlandi

www.rossanaorlandi.com
Rossana's Milan shop is an Aladdin's cave of yummyness, set in a beautiful courtyard. Check out the visionary homeware store, and be sure to grab a coffee or lunch in her little place next door.

USA

ABC Carpet & Home (USA)

www.abchome.com
This vast store is full to the brim with stuff for the home, from tableware to lighting to furniture, not to mention the rugs.

Jonathan Adler

www.jonathanadler.com
Jonathan Adler put humour into homeware Stateside with his happy, joyful accessories and furniture. I salute him!

John Derian

www.johnderian.com
John Derian is the king of decoupage, and his trays, plates and paper weights are amazing as gifts. His stores sell textiles, lighting and furniture, which he has either sourced globally or made under his own label.

Kelly Wearstler

www.kellywearstler.com
Kelly's designs are sold to cool department stores and boutiques around the world but if you happen to be in LA pop into her flagship store. From homeware to fashion, the vibe is jaw-droopingly cool. Hip, glam, boundary pushing!

Michele Varian

www.michelevarian.com
I'm a big fan of this New York homeware designer. Great for decorative pillows, glassware, home accessories and a little quirk – at a wide range of prices.

Olde Good Things

www.ogtstore.com
Architectural items, altered antiques, farm tables, industrial stuff and the best vintage tin tiles on the planet (believe me, I've searched!). They ship all over the world and certainly on the tile front nothing I've come across is as good.

Saipua

www.saipua.com
The coolest florist in NYC (located in Brooklyn): sells country-esque blooms put together with absolute finesse.

Schoolhouse Electric

www.schoolhouseelectric.com
Schoolhouse specialises in classic period, vintage and contemporary light fixtures, as well as home accessories and furniture. I love them for their lighting, which is beautifully crafted and elegant.

Second Hand Rose

www.secondhandrose.com
A totally fabulous vintage wallpaper source: the collection ranges from chinoiserie to damask to faux finishes. And they ship all over the world.

Terrain at Stylers

www.shopterrain.com
Magical pretty much sums up Terrain. Owned by Urban Outfitters, it resembles a ramshackle greenhouse and specialises in garden and home décor, artisan foods, gifts – the whole shebang. If you ever get the chance to go to the brick-and-mortar stores, block out at least two hours!

West Elm

www.westelm.com
Super modern and affordable, West Elm offers a vast selection of products for the home, from rugs to sofas.

ANTIQUES

Alfies
alfiesantiques.com
This indoor market is one of the coolest places to buy vintage in London. Pretty pricey, but if you're looking for something special, this is the place to go.

Atomic Antiques
www.atomica.me.uk
Atomic Antiques in east London has a beautiful selection of vintage finds. The owner has the best eye in town.

International Antiques & Collectors Fairs (IACF)
www.iacf.co.uk/fairs
Europe's largest antiques and collectables events, held every other month. Out of town, but well worth the long haul. I mostly go to Ardingly and Newark. The trick is to go on trade day. You'll pay £20 to get in but come visitors' day (the day after) all the best stuff is gone.

Kempton
www.sunburyantiques.com
A twice-monthly market (every other Tuesday), you will find me here most times, wrapped in the thickest of coats with pyjamas underneath in winter, since I need to get up at 4.30 a.m. to get there! And that's the key. Get there at the get-go, 6.30 a.m. with a torch, to find the bargains.

ONLINE BARGAINS

Gumtree and Preloved
www.gumtree.com
www.preloved.co.uk
Classified sites can be great for tables, chairs and other second-hand furniture. These two are reasonably priced, plus you plug in your local area to cut down the expense of getting items couriered across the country.

Salvo
www.salvo.co.uk
You can buy anything here, from an old barn in Wales to a rustic old kitchen sink. A great resource for salvaged pieces, and the prices are not outlandish.

FLEA MARKETS

Les Puces de Saint-Ouen (Paris)
marcheauxpuces-saintouen.com
The most famous flea in Paris is the one at Porte de Clignancourt. Covering seven hectares (which is huge!), it's the largest antiques market in the world, receiving up to 180,000 visitors each weekend. It's also expensive, so if you're looking for a bargain, steer clear. Huge chandeliers from old country estates and some truly beautiful retro finds are all on display.

Porte de Vanves (Paris)
pucesdevanves.typepad.com
This weekend flea market near the Porte de Vanves metro stop is the oldest in Paris. Set amongst magnificent old plane trees, it's a heavenly place to visit and less touristy than Clingnancourt. You have to barter; don't let the language put you off! I've come away with paintings, old leather chairs, dining chairs (which somehow I managed to smuggle back on to the Eurostar!), and a huge chandelier.

Brooklyn Flea (NYC)
www.brooklynflea.com
Part vintage bazaar, part hipster hang out, Brooklyn Flea features hundreds of great vendors, plus delicious artisan food stalls. It's also worth pottering around the streets of Williamsburg to check out the indie stores that have set up home here.

Hell's Kitchen and Chelsea Flea Market (NYC)
www.annexmarkets.com
If you're in New York, these flea markets are a must-visit, full of vintage fabrics, rugs, furniture, every type of fine silver item imaginable, and more.

PAINT

I buy paint samples like other people buy shoes; nothing sets my heart a-racing more then a new paint colour on the market. In fact, I love it so much I developed my own paint range. It started with grabbing some of my mother's old pastels and playing around with various hues. Then, with my sister Gemma (a partner in the biz), I found an old art supply store in Paris (La Maison du Pastel), which once created colours for Degas and Whistler, and spent the most amazing day there, overwhelmed by the pastels' intensity. Their dry crayon-like sticks create a distinctive cloudy texture on paper, and that was the finish I wanted to create.

It took an age to get it right, but I think we've nailed it! Our range has the same richness the pastels have in the murkiest, muddiest swampiest colours. The browns have undertones of black; the olive has undertones of brown; then there is a zingy Amazon parrot-type green; and a red with so so so much black in it that at certain times of the day you're not sure whether it is black or red! They are mysterious, seductive and pretty darn life changing!

You can find the full range of paints on my website (www.abigailahern.org).

I'm also a big fan of the following paints. Yes, some are a little expensive, but the pigmentation has far more depth, and is worth every penny in my book.

Annie Sloan
www.anniesloan.com

Fired Earth
www.firedearth.com

Farrow & Ball
www.farrow-ball.com

Marston & Langiner
www.marston-and-langinger.com

Little Greene Paint Company
www.littlegreene.com

Zoffany
www.zoffany.com

Paint Library
www.paint-library.co.uk

Papers and Paints
www.papers-paints.co.uk

COLOURFUL READS

www.designspongeonline.com
Design Sponge is great if you're looking for some inspirational DIY projects. And if you fancy launching a business of your own, Grace Bonney's Biz Ladies makes for pretty cool reading, and her Before and Afters are inspirational.

www.desiretoinspire.net
A joint blog run by two interior design junkies, this is a visual feast of ideas, very well presented.

www.thedesignfiles.net
I like the cross section of topics covered, from homes to retail to food to craft, and I dip into it every week.

www.domainehome.com
I love Domaine: stylishly curated, full of daily inspirational tips and tricks from home tours to deco ideas.

eye-swoon.com
Athena Calderone has one of the coolest apartments on the planet, located in Brooklyn NYC, which we are very privileged to include in this book. She also pens the blog eye-swoon.com: a fab destination for all things relating to design, food and creativity in general.

www.myvibemylife.com
Kelly Wearstler has a global lifestyle brand under her belt as well as being known for her boundary pushing designs. Her blog curates all the amazing inspiring images she comes across on her travels as well as highlighting her incredible

AUSTRALIA
Porter's Paints
www.porterspaints.com.au

Murobond
www.murobond.com.au

BELGIUM
Flamant
www.flamantpaint.com

Emery & Cie
www.emeryetcie.com

FRANCE
Ressources
www.ressource-decoration.com

USA
Benjamin Moore
www.benjaminmooore.com

Ralph Lauren
www.ralphlaurenhome.com

Martha Stewart Living Paint
www.homedepot.com

Sherwin Williams
www.sherwin-williams.com

projects. Her designs are jaw dropping. I am so flattered and delighted to showcase her home in my book.

www.roselandgreene.blogspot. co.uk
I like the images on this blog. Rather than just rehashing what's in the latest magazine, the choice is considered and always interesting – from a cool pad in Paris to a loft in NYC.

www.saipua.blogspot.co.uk
The most amazing florist in NYC chronicles her blooms and her experiences. Funny, straight from the heart, and I can relate in so many ways to the trials and tribulations, the highs and lows of running a business.

www.theinteriorsaddict.com
Interiors, style, and personality profiles from a stylish Sydney-based Brit.

www.theselby.com
Hip photographer Todd Selby shoots interesting people in their personal spaces, in a very relaxed way. I adore the shots he did of my pad not so long ago. Very natural, uber laid back, he uses only natural daylight so in some cases the images he shoots almost look like paintings. Adore!

www.sfgirlbybay.com
'Bohemian modern' style from a San Francisco-based blogger, photographer, stylist and flea market queen. Kind of makes me want to up sticks and move to San Fran.

MAGAZINES

I subscribe to many interiors magazines around the world, including: *Elle Decoration* and *Livingetc* in the UK; www. lonnymag.com (a bimonthly online interiors magazine); *Real Living*, *Inside Out*, *Belle* and *Vogue Living* from Australia; and from Italy, *Casa Vogue* and *Elle Decor Italia*.

PINTEREST

Pinterest.com is a completely addictive site that you can use to create virtual mood and design boards. Pin images that you love – cool products, design ideas and inspiration – from anywhere on the web, to bring all the elements of your style together. Create your own Pinterest boards, or follow other Pinterest users and 'repin' their pins, too. Hours of fun!

INDEX

Page numbers in *italic* refer to the captions

THANK YOUS

I am deeply thankful to Helen Lewis and Anne Furniss for giving me the opportunity to write this fabulous new tome. Who would have thought, twenty-odd years ago when we all first started working in publishing together, that it would lead to this, my third and most fabulous book yet? Thank you so much guys!

To Nicola Ellis, who has done such an amazing job with the design of the book, thank you Nikki. To Zelda Turner, my editor, who has read through pages of my yabberings, laid the book out so beautifully and been so supportive throughout.

This book wouldn't look like this if it hadn't been for the spectacular photography of Graham Atkins-Hughes. I am in awe of the way you play with light, take the most incredible pictures and make me laugh on some of the longest days!

The hugest thank you to everyone who loaned us their fabulous homes to shoot in: designers Alina Preciado, Athena Calderone, Jean-Louis Deniot, Kelly Wearstler, Kyle Schuneman and Sue Miller; hospitality maven Brent Bolthouse; journalist Kelley Carter; and lighting designer Michelle James.

Thank you also to designer Mariska Meijers, who supplied photographs of her beautiful apartment, photographed by Joanne Zonderland; and also to designer Sarah Lavoine for photographs of her Parisian apartment, by Francis Amiand.

To my fabulous team – Alex, Craig, David, Katherine and Rebecca – I am deeply thankful for all your hard work and passion. To Gem & Russ: the AA story is only the success it is because of you two guys who play such an integral part in forming it. Gem, there are simply not enough thanks yous in the world.

To my family, firstly my two little nieces Lilly and Thea who can't quite read yet, I love you guys. To my parents, for always being so supportive and upbeat, and to Gillian and Alan for all your incredible support. Love love love you! To Holly & Lee, who I never see enough of, but from this year on will make more time as it's all passing so quickly.

Lastly to my little family: Graham, my husband, who is never grumpy, always optimistic and who works the craziest hours believing in this business like no one else I know. To the two Ms, of course (an integral part of my life): without their shenanigans I doubt I would laugh as much as I do. And, most importantly, to you guys, to all my amazing customers, blog & social media readers. Thank you for your unrelenting, incredible support, words of cheer, encouragement and feedback. You motivate me to constantly push and grow this business. Thank you all so much!

Editorial director: Anne Furniss
Art director: Helen Lewis
Project editor: Zelda Turner
Designer: Nicola Ellis
Photography: Graham Atkins-Hughes
Production: Vincent Smith, Tom Moore

First published in 2015 by Quadrille Publishing Ltd
Pentagon House, 52–54 Southwark Street, London SE1 1UN
www.quadrille.co.uk

Quadrille is an imprint of Hardie Grant
www.hardiegrant.com.au

Text © Abigail Ahern 2015
Design and layout © Quadrille Publishing Limited 2015
Photography © Graham Atkins-Hughes 2015

All book rights reserved. No part of this book may be reproduced, stored in a retrieval system or transmitted in any form or by any means, electronic, electrostatic, magnetic tape, mechanical, photocopying, recording or otherwise, without the prior permission in writing from the publisher.

A catalogue record of this book is available from the British Library.

ISBN: 978 184949 581 3
Printed and bound in China.